ALSO BY JULIE DE VERE HUNT

Apostle to Mary Magdalene
Mary Magdalene's Legacy

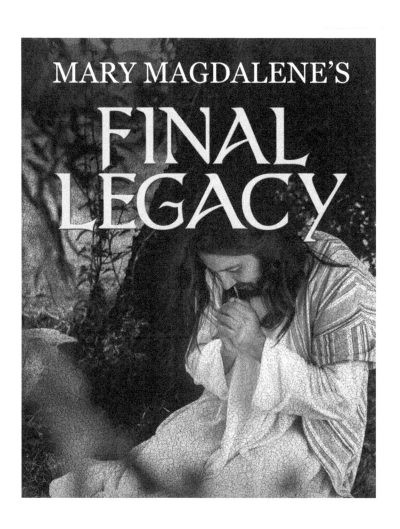

MARY MAGDALENE'S

FINAL LEGACY

JULIE DE VERE HUNT

First published in the UK in 2020 © Julie de Vere Hunt

Website: www.marymagdaleneslegacy.com

Email: marymagdaleneslegacy@gmail.com

Facebook: marymagdaleneslegacy

Instagram: juliedvhunt

Twitter: juliedeverehunt

© G2 Rights Ltd. www.g2books.co.uk

Printed and bound in Europe

ISBN: 978 1 78281 592 1

This book is dedicated to
Ratu Bagus
and all his students; those who live at the ashram,
but also all those around the world,
who are dedicating their lives to serve as light workers, at this
critical time in humanity.
One day their efforts will be recognized and appreciated.

Om Swastiastu Ratu Bagus

ACKNOWLEDGEMENTS

It is impossible to list everyone who has helped me put this book together, and I thank each and every one of them from the centre of my heart. I have not named you, but you know who you are!

In particular I would like to thank Ratu's students, especially those I have met and interacted with at the ashram in Bali, for their invaluable insights and experiences. I believe the issues and dynamics that exist in a community today, are very similar to those experienced in communities two thousand years ago. We are all human beings, then and now.

It is certainly not an easy option choosing to live in a community; the courage, devotion and discipline shown by Ratu's long term students, both Balinese and Western, have earned my utmost respect and deep gratitude.

I would not be here today without my parents, Michael and Jean Adams, who gave me and my three brothers, the best start in life I could have wished for. Only now I have my own family do I appreciate the love and sacrifices they made for us.

I am blessed with a loving, supportive husband and three children who encourage me even though they might not always agree with me. My children have been my greatest teachers, and kept my feet firmly on the ground!

And finally, Ratu Bagus, your love, humility and desire to help humanity, never ceases to amaze me.

CONTENTS

CONTENTS continued

PART 1: THE LIFE OF JUDE

Grandson of Jesus and Mary Magdalene

PROLOGUE

September 108, Lake Mareotis, Alexandria, Egypt

My name will forever be associated with betrayal...

I was born in Gaul in 63, shortly after my grandmother Mary Magdalene died. My name was chosen by my mother, Sarah, in memory of the apostle Judas Iscariot, who was wrongly accused of betraying Yeshua*. Judas was greatly revered in our family. Mary Magdalene wrote about him in both her diary and in *The Gospel of Thomas* (Codex II), where Judas predicted his own death. Sarah wrote *The Gospel of Judas* (Codex V) as a tribute to him.

I was known to my family as Jude.

My mother Sarah, was the daughter of Yeshua and Mary Magdalene, which makes me their first grandson. My older sisters, Mary and Anne, chose not to marry, so it was on my shoulders to carry on the bloodline of Yeshua.

Mary Magdalene founded the *Therapeutae* community at Lake Mareotis, just outside Alexandria in 33, which was where my mother Sarah was born later that year. When Sarah was nine years old they had to flee to Gaul in a boat, after they had been betrayed to the Roman authorities.

They lived there happily for twenty years until my grandmother's death in 63. This is where my mother met and married my father, Jean Claude, a native of Gaul.

After my grandmother died in 63, my parents sailed from Gaul to Alexandria with me and my two older sisters. I was just two months old. Sarah said this was Mary Magdalene's wish, so that Sarah could carry on her work in Alexandria.

Jean Claude was a cabinet maker, of some repute, and when I think

* Yeshua is known today as Jesus

of him, I can still smell the wood chippings and glue he used in making his pieces. I would spend hours with him in his workshop, watching him work. I wanted to be like him.

When I was seven I was able to join my sisters at the esteemed Serapeum school. We were some of the few Jewish children at the Serapeum; Mother had petitioned the Roman Governor of Egypt, Tiberius Julius Alexander, for us to be admitted. She was granted an audience because his uncle, Philo, had been Mother's tutor at Lake Mareotis. Like her mother, Mary Magdalene, she was a determined woman and did not take no for an answer.

My sisters were good students and worked hard; I enjoyed the sport and entertained my peers by acting the goat. I passed all my exams, but I was more interested in finishing my schoolwork, so I could join my father in his workshop.

In July 81, when I was eighteen and had finished school, Sarah, Mary and Anne moved to Lake Mareotis. I wanted to stay in Alexandria with my father Jean Claude to apprentice as a cabinet maker. This took four years. I was in no hurry to go and live at the community.

This is when I fell in with a group of heathen friends who enjoyed drinking, gambling, women... The alcohol was the worst; I would get drunk and boast about my commissions to rich Jews, overcharging them, taking advantage of my heritage, as well as trading on my father's reputation as a first class cabinet maker.

I fell in love with a married Greek woman, Alexa. It was lust actually. She was bored and I was full of testosterone. And she was unavailable, which of course made her all the more alluring. We wrote letters to one another - nothing actually happened, but her husband found one of my letters.

In Greek society, absolutely *anything* is permissible regarding sex, bar adultery with another man's wife, as she is considered his property. If you were caught, the punishment was performed in the agora. A mullet or large radish, would be rammed up the place the sun doesn't shine...for the amusement of the crowds. The thought of this was inconceivable - I wouldn't be able to face my family and my business would be over. I was so distraught I even considered throwing myself off the top of Pharos Lighthouse, but I was a coward too...

After yet another drunken night, I stumbled home. But the drink had not numbed my feelings of shame and self-loathing. In fact it made it worse. I collapsed on the floor, and began to sob. I cried out, begging for help from God, Yeshua, the angels, whoever was prepared to listen. To my astonishment, a light appeared in the corner of my room, and then I heard a voice. I felt an unfamiliar feeling of peace slowly wash over me. The voice told me to leave the city immediately, to travel to Rome, to see Pope Clement of Rome.

The leader of the Christian church? Are you kidding? The voice was insistent and I was desperate...

I had to get out of Alexandria - so what did I have to lose?

Chapter I

Pope Clement I of Rome

July 85

On the voyage to Rome I had plenty of time to reflect on my shameful behaviour that had driven me out of my own city. Inside I had a deep sense of insecurity, a fear of failure of not being able to live up to all that was expected of me. I was full of self-pity, dread and doubt about my visit to Clement in Rome. How could he possibly help?

I arrived on a Sunday afternoon and the tolling church bells led me to Saint Peter's church. I slipped into the back and sat on an empty church pew wondering what I should do next. I was weary so I closed my eyes and prayed thanks to God for my safe arrival in Rome. I may have had doubts, but I had not lost my faith entirely... When I opened my eyes I was greeted with the sight of a middle aged man of the church smiling at me. He was modestly dressed in a dark brown tunic tied with a leather thong. It did not occur to me even for a second that this was Pope Clement.

"You must be Jude du Bois - I have been expecting you for some days." I looked at him quizzically.

"Ah yes, I heard of your visit just over a week or so ago?" I lowered my head with relief; at least I would not have to explain why I was here.

"Give me a moment whilst I ask one of my presbyters to take over from my church duties. Then I will be able to escort you to my lodgings."

I liked this man immediately. He personified non-judgement. I was struck by his humility - he insisted on me calling him Clement, saying he was unused to any pomp or formality associated with being Pope.

His housemaid prepared us a simple supper of soup and bread and we talked long into the evening.

I asked him how he came to Yeshua. It was quite a tall story!

Born of noble Roman stock, his father was called Faustinianus and his mother Macidiana. He had twin brothers called Faustinus and Faustus. Macidiana was strikingly beautiful, and her husband's brother lusted after her, although this was unrequited. She dared not confide in her husband, for fear of causing animosity between the two men. She had a crazy idea that if she went away for a while until this illicit attention had had time to cool, all would be well. So she invented a dream, which she related to Faustinianus as follows,

"In my dream, I saw a man standing beside me ordering me to leave the city as soon as possible, taking the twins with me and staying away until he told me to return. If I did not comply with his wishes, the twins and I would all die!" Faustinianus was superstitious and so sent his wife and twin sons, with a large retinue, to live in Athens. He kept his youngest son, Clement, with him to keep him company.

The mother and twins sailed away, but one night a storm blew up and they were ship-wrecked. Macidiana became separated from her sons and was washed up on a rocky island. She feared the boys had drowned and became inconsolable; she cried and screamed and tore her hands with her teeth. Many women tried to help her, but to no avail.

Then one woman told her that her own husband, still a young man, also drowned at sea and for love of him she refused to remarry. She invited Macidiana to stay with her, earning her keep by mending and sewing. But in a short time her badly damaged hands lost all feeling and she was unable to work.

Furthermore, the kind woman who took her in became bedridden. So Macidiana was forced to beg on the streets.

A year had passed with no word since Macidiana and the twins had left Rome - her husband sent messengers to look for them in Athens, but the messengers found no trace of his family. Finally, Faustinianus left his son Clement in the care of tutors, and boarded a ship to look for his wife and sons. But fate served another cruel blow and he was also shipwrecked.

So young Clement spent the next twenty years believing he had no family. He threw himself into his studies, passing all his exams with distinction. He had an unquenchable thirst for philosophy, as he desperately wished to discover the soul was immortal. This sadly eluded him.

Then Barnabas came to Rome to preach the Christian faith. The philosophers decided he was a fool; Clement the philosopher mocked and scorned his preaching and posed a question in order to ridicule him,

"The mosquito is a tiny animal. Why does it have six feet and wings as well, whereas the elephant, a huge beast, has no wings and only four feet?" Barnabas replied,

"Foolish fellow, I could very easily answer your question if you were asking it in order to learn the truth; but it would be absurd to talk to you about creatures, since you know nothing of the One who makes all living creatures. As you do not know the Creator, how can you possibly understand his creatures!"

These words so touched the heart of Clement the philosopher that he asked Barnabus for instruction in the Christian faith. On Barnabas' suggestion, he then hurried to Judea to visit Peter. The apostle completed his instruction in the faith of Christ and gave him clear proof of the soul's immortality.

Peter asked Clement about his family and he relayed the whole sad tale. Peter could not restrain his tears and wished to help find Clement's family. He and his disciples, Aquilas and Nicetas, were guided to Tartus, Syria, and from there to an island called Aradus where Macidiana lived. Shortly after arriving, Peter and his disciples were approached by a beggar woman. Peter asked her why she did not work and she replied,

"My hands are so weakened by me biting them that I wish I had drowned along with my sons!"

"Do not say that! Did you not know that the souls of those who end their own lives are punished severely?"

"If only I could be sure that souls live after death, I would gladly kill myself so I could be with my sons!"

Peter invited her to tell him the whole story of how she ended up as a beggar on this island. When she had finished he nodded knowingly, and replied,

"There is a young man named Clement with us - he told me a very similar story of what happened to his mother and brothers."

Macidiana froze for a moment and then threw herself at Peter's feet, begging him to let her see her son. Peter led her to the ship where Clement was. Clement saw Peter approaching with a woman hand in hand, and Clement began to laugh; Macidiana rushed towards Clement and hugged him kissing him repeatedly. Clement thought she was mad, and pushed her away indignantly. Peter said calmly,

"Clement, what are you doing? Why do you push your mother away!"

Despite the years that had passed and hardship she had endured, Clement recognized his mother and dropped down beside the prostate woman, weeping tears of joy. Then Peter asked his disciples to bring the paralyzed woman who had befriended Macidiana, and cured her immediately. Macidiana asked about her husband and Peter replied,

"He left Rome looking for you and never returned."

At this she sighed, as the great joy at finding her son was suddenly outweighed by the grief of losing her husband and twin sons.

At this point Nicetas and Aquilas appeared and asked who the woman was. "Who is this?" they asked. Clement answered them,

"This is my mother, who our Lord has returned to me with the help of Peter, my master". Peter then told them all that happened. Nicetas and Aquilas stood up, shaken to the core, and said,

"Oh Lord, is what we have heard a dream, or is it true?" Peter replied,

"My sons, we are not raving mad! What you heard is true!" The two young men rubbed their eyes and cried,

"We are Faustinus and Faustus, and our mother thought we were lost at sea!" They rushed to embrace their mother and covered her face in kisses. It was too much for Macidiana to take in - she looked at Peter and said,

"What is the meaning of this?" Peter replied smiling,

"These are your sons, Faustinus and Faustus, who you thought had drowned at sea!" Macidiana was filled with so much joy she fainted and when she came to she said,

"My darling sons, tell me how you escaped?"

"When the ship broke up, we clung to a plank, and some pirates picked us up. They changed our names and sold us to an honest widow called Justina, who treated us as her own sons and had us educated in liberal studies. We met Simon Magus in philosophy school and joined him. In time, we saw through his deceit and through Zacheus, were introduced to Peter and became his disciples.

The following day Peter took the three brothers off to a secluded place to pray. A poor old man approached them and said,

"I pity you brothers! There is no God. Everything is controlled by chance and the position of the planets at the time of your birth. I have studied astrology and am sure of this. I know the horoscope of my wife and I, and what they determined for each of us, actually happened. At her birth she had Mars with Venus above the centre, the moon in descent in the house of Mars and in the borders of Saturn. This alignment makes women commit adultery, fall in love with their slaves, travel to distant parts, and perish in the sea. All of this happened. I cannot blame her for any of this, as the stars compelled her to do this."

The old man went on to tell them about her dream, and how she and the children had perished in the shipwreck. His sons were poised to throw themselves upon him and tell what really happened, but Peter restrained them. He turned to the old man and said,

"If I can deliver your wife, who has remained faithful to you, along with your three sons, will you believe there is nothing to astrology?" The old man replied,

"You cannot possibly do what you have promised, as it is impossible anything can happen outside the influence of the stars!" Peter said to him,

"Look! Here is your son Clement, and here are your twin sons, Faustinus and Faustus!" The old man collapsed to the ground - his sons bent over him and kissed him, fearing he had died of shock. He recovered and heard every detail of what had happened to them. Then suddenly, Macidiana appeared weeping, crying out,

"Is this my husband?" Her husband ran to her, shedding copious tears as the whole family was reunited.

Soon after, a messenger arrived to tell them that one of Caesar's ministers had arrived in Antioch to hunt down all magicians and put them to death. Simon Magus, out of hatred for the two brothers who had been his disciples and left him, impressed his own likeness on Faustinianus' face so he would be taken for Simon Magus, and the emperors' ministers would arrest and execute Faustinianus.

Simon had made some salve and applied it to Faustinianus' face while he slept, and by using magic, imposed his own likeness upon him.

Simon disappeared to allow his plan to materialise. When Faustinianus went back to his sons and Peter, the sons were terrified to see Simon's face and yet hear their father's voice. Peter was the only one who saw who he really was and said,

"Why are you cursing your father and running from him?" Faustinianus mournfully said,

"What has happened to me that in the course of one day I am reunited with my own wife and sons, and now they do not recognize me?"

While Simon Magus was in Antioch, he had turned the local people against Peter, calling him a sorcerer and a murderer. Peter then said to Faustinianus,

"Since you look like Simon, go to Antioch and retract everything he has said against me. Then I will come to Antioch and, in front of everyone, restore your own face to you!"

When Faustinianus had carried out Peter's instructions, the apostle arrived and prayed over him, completely eradicating the likeness of Simon from him. The people of Antioch welcomed Peter with much honour, raising him to the bishop's chair.

Unaware his plan had been foiled, Simon Magus arrived in Antioch and was met with hostility by the local people. He was chased out of the city, never to return.

The sons instructed their parents in the faith and Peter baptized them. Shortly after, they all travelled to Rome, where Faustinianus and his family finally returned to their family home.

It was the most incredible story I had ever heard in my life, and yet I believed every word from this humble, modest man. I sat there in silence, trying to digest all he had told me. I turned to Clement and said,

"And how did you become the Pope, the leader of the Christian Church?" Clement replied that when Peter knew his end was imminent, he wished to appoint Clement as his successor. Peter said Clement had journeyed with Peter from beginning to end and had heard all his homilies. He had found him above all others, steadfast in his faith, pious, learned, chaste, good, upright and warm-hearted.

But Clement felt unworthy, and apologetically expressed his reluctance to accept the bishop's office. Peter had to convince him,

"When has Christ need of you? Now, when the wicked one has sworn against His bride, or in the future, when He is victorious and no need of further help? Is it not obvious to all that it is now? Show me a better man than yourself, and I will leave you in peace!"

Clement had no choice but to accept and slowly bowed his head as a sign of consent. Peter smiled as he realized he had won Clement over and said,

"When I depart from this life, send to James the Just an account of how you have journeyed with me, hearing my discourses in every city, and witnessed my deeds. He will be comforted greatly when he learns that you, Clement, will be my successor."

When Peter died, Clement followed his predecessor's instructions to the letter. He wrote *"Clement's Epitome of the Popular Sermons of Peter"* and dispatched them to James in Jerusalem. A note accompanied the letter, asking James to call the elders and read it to them. Clement also urged the teachings to be shared only with those who had been through initiation and probation.

Clement, a farsighted man, took precautions for the future. He foresaw that future popes may take Peter's example and install their own choice as successor.

So Clement conceded his papacy first to Linus, and then to Cletus.

After them, Clement was elected to preside. He was so obviously a good and holy man, that he was well liked by Jews, Gentiles and Christians alike. He did not wish his flock to be subject to the humiliation of beggary, as his mother had been, and drew up a list of poor Christians in the provinces who had been baptized, and ensured they were given alms by the church. This was in the form of a meal after the Eucharist prayer.

I sat there, feeling very small indeed. And yet I did not feel judged. Clement put his arm on my shoulder and said,

"Jude, your soul is in conflict with your body and mind, but all is not lost - your heart is open. The Lord has great plans for you! You have been sent to me; I am your shepherd, here to protect you and guide you in any way I can, if you will allow me?" I looked at him, full of uncertainty,

"What can I do to get rid of all these nagging doubts I have?" I implored.

"Fast, spend time alone in nature, and pray. Have faith, trust and be patient. You will be guided." Clement made it sound so simple.

I left the next day for the country, walking along the Via Campana. I did not have to wait long - I had my first vision that day, as clear as anything. It seemed so real... I had four more visions in the course of the year I spent with Clement.

I wrote them down and called them *"The Shepherd of Hermas"*: Hermas is the narrator and hero of the narrative. The Shepherd is the divine teacher, who communicates to Hermas, either by general rules of behaviour or allegory, the lessons which were to be written down in a book and used for the instruction of the Church. The book comprises the five visions, twelve commandments, and ten parables. I was instructed to make three copies of the book; one for Clement, so he could preach it in foreign cities, another to Grapte, who was to preach to the widows and orphans, and one for me to instruct the presbyters here in Rome.

In all the time I stayed with Clement I never saw him fall from grace

- Peter had made a wise choice. He had set me back on the path and my faith was restored.

Clement asked me what my plans were for the immediate future. I said I was awaiting a sign. Clement suggested I visit John the Evangelist, the only surviving apostle of Yeshua, who was living in exile on the Greek island of Patmos. I had told Clement about how he had betrayed my grandmother, Mary Magdalene, many years ago. Clement just smiled, gave me a knowing look and handed me a letter,

"Take this letter of introduction with you - John can be a little hot-headed."

Chapter II

John the Evangelist

May 86 Patmos, the Aegean Sea

John the Evangelist had been banished to the island of Patmos by the Emperor Domitian in April 82, for preaching the Word of our Lord in Ephesus.

I had some reservations about visiting John, but Clement was confident his letter, together with my persuasive powers, would warm John to me. After all, it was over 40 years since Mary and her entourage had had to flee Egypt.

I boarded a ship at Puteoli to make the voyage to Patmos, a small, rocky island in the Aegean Sea, off the west coast of Asia Minor. One of the northernmost islands of the Dodecanese complex. Just 13 square miles, it should not be difficult to find John.

We sailed into Skala and I asked the locals where John was living. Clement had told me he was living in a cave as a hermit, communing day and night with our Lord. I had also heard he was well received by the islanders; Patmos was only 65 miles from Ephesus, and news of numerous miracles he had performed there had travelled to Patmos. He roved around the island preaching to the locals when he felt called to do so.

A fisherman directed me to the cave where John lived - it was located on a hill a short distance from Skala on the way to Chora.

John was accompanied by his faithful disciple Prochorus. Prochorus was one of the 72 disciples of Yeshua, and after the crucifixion elected as one of the seven deacons responsible for the care of the poor Christians in Jerusalem. When John went to Ephesus in 48, he asked Prochorus to accompany him in his mission to establish a Christian community there.

John did not arrive in Patmos as a defeated exile or as a political prisoner, but as a servant of our Lord on a spiritual mission, continuing to preach the Word of our Lord.

I approached the cave with some trepidation and called out so as not to startle them. Prochorus, a man of 70 or so - slight, with grey hair and a straggly beard, was the first to appear to see who I was. When I gave him my name, and said I had been sent by Pope Clement I of Rome, he dropped his guard and welcomed me wholeheartedly. John, aged 85 or so, emerged behind him, supported by a staff. He hugged me and indicated for me to sit on a smooth rock at the cave entrance.

"Welcome to our humble home, young man. I do not encourage visitors, as I prefer to spend my days in silence so I can listen to our Lord, but as you have such an esteemed introduction and have travelled far, I am happy to make an exception!"

John did not question me further as to my origins, which was probably for the best - I did not know how he would react to me being Mary Magdalene's grandson. He was eager to tell me about his visions since being on Patmos,

John related that early on during his stay, a triple fissure appeared in the rock, through which light and sound could enter the cave. To John, these symbolized the Holy Trinity. John was convinced he heard the voice of God,

"On the Lord's Day I was in the Spirit, and I heard behind me a loud voice like a trumpet, which said:

'Write on a scroll what you see and send it to the seven churches: Ephesus, Smyrna, Pergamum, Thyatira, Sardis, Philadelphia and Laodicea.'

I turned around to see the voice that was speaking to me. And when I turned I saw seven golden lampstands, and among the lampstands was someone like a son of man, dressed in a robe reaching down to his feet and with a golden sash around his chest.

The hair on his head was white like wool, as white as snow, and his eyes were like blazing fire. His feet were like bronze glowing in a furnace, and his voice was like the sound of rushing waters. In his right hand he held seven stars. His face was like the sun shining in all its brilliance.

When I saw him I fell at his feet as though dead. Then he placed his right hand on me and said:

"Do not be afraid. I am the First and the Last. I am the Living One; I was dead, and now look, I am alive for ever and ever!

Write, therefore what you have seen, what is now and what will take place later. The mystery of the seven stars and the seven golden lampstands is this; the seven stars are the angels of the seven churches, and the seven lampstands are the seven churches."

John named these transmissions *The Revelation**, which comes from the Greek word *apokalypsis*, and means 'unveiling', or 'revealing' of divine mysteries.

The number seven represents perfection in ancient numerology.

After the introductory letter to the seven churches, John describes a series of prophetic visions, including figures such as the Seven Headed Dragon, The Serpent and the Beast, a New Jerusalem descending from heaven, and the Second Coming of Yeshua.

Although addressed to the seven churches, it is clearly for a wider audience, and I recognized the allegorical and multi-layered form of encryption.

John was concerned about the conflict within the Christian community of Asia Minor over whether to engage in, or withdraw from the far larger non-Christian community who laid allegiance to the Roman cult of empire. Defiance against Roman society could result in death; *Revelation* offered solace and victory over this reality by offering an apocalyptic hope for the future.

*The Book of Revelation is the last book of the New Testament and thus the final book of the Christian Bible.

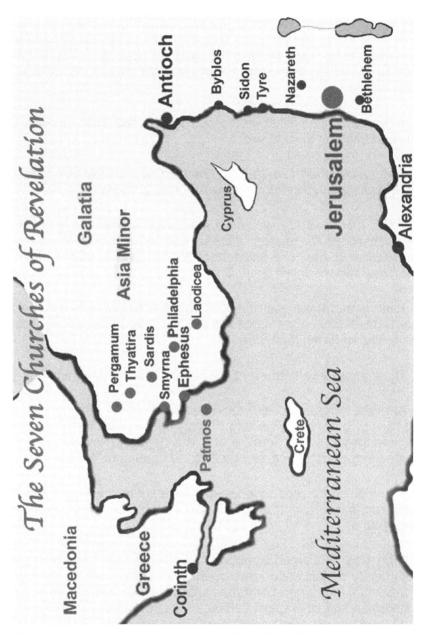

Figure 1: Map showing the Seven Churches of Asia Minor (Turkey)

On another level, *Revelation* is an allegory of the individual's spiritual path and the ongoing struggle between good and evil; experienced by each and every one of us. The fight between light and dark, both inside us and out in the world.

I felt I could learn much from listening to John and Prochorus, but felt uneasy about not telling them who I was. If I did not say anything they might never ask; on the other hand if I did tell them, John might refuse to speak to me. More importantly, our Lord could see I was not being true to myself - that bothered me far more than anything John or Prochorus could do or say, so in the end I just blurted it out...

"I am the son of Sarah, daughter of Mary Magdalene and Yeshua. I am the only grandson of Mary Magdalene and Yeshua; I have two older sisters who live with my parents at Lake Mareotis, Alexandria."

Time seemed to stand still as I was bombarded with stunned silence. As they turned to me I saw their faces were drained of all colour. John had been called 'son of thunder' when he was younger, and I feared the worst. Prochurus said nothing, and after what felt like an eternity John stood up and said, with his voice simmering with rage,

"You should have told me this earlier - it is best you leave now. I have nothing further to discuss with you." Prochurus stared uncomfortably at the ground while John looked as if he might explode. I rose quickly to my feet. I kept my cool and said to John,

"I apologize for having disturbed your peace. Whatever happened, that still distresses you so much even to this day, was a long time ago and nothing to do with me." I picked up my bag and promptly left. Prochurus called after me,

"You will find lodgings in Skala - go to the Fisherman's Inn in the harbour".

It was not dark yet, so I made my way down the hill to Skala, the port I had arrived at earlier that day. I located the Fisherman's Inn and secured a room for the night. I did not feel like eating, and went to my room to pray. My mind was very busy, I should not have listened to Clement - John was never going to change his mind.

I awoke early the next morning to hear voices outside my bedroom window. I peered outside and could see the locals making their way to the market square. I quickly dressed and asked the innkeeper what was happening. He said that John had arrived to preach in the market square. This was something I could not miss, despite his animosity towards me. I watched him make his way down the path, followed by an ever increasing entourage. He was greeted by everyone; old and young, men and women, children laughing, with dogs barking excitedly. Women appeared from doorways offering him alms, but he just waved them cheerfully away, profusely thanking each and every one of them. He made his way to the market square and prepared to start preaching from *Revelation*.

A crowd quickly assembled - they did not know when he would appear again, and clearly did not want to miss an opportunity to hear his teachings. This 85 year old man seemed much more vital and larger in stature than the man I had met briefly the day before. He loudly and passionately delivered his message - such heart and faith kept the audience spellbound. He spoke with such passion and truth I was moved to tears. I saw John notice me amongst the hundreds of people. He spoke for over an hour before Prochorus led him away for some refreshment.

I slowly returned to the inn to collect my belongings. I was unsure of where I would go next, but there was no reason for me to stay any longer as my mission here had failed. I was settling my bill with the innkeeper when the door burst open. It was Prochorus - my surprise was met with his delight. Still out of breath, he gasped,

"Thank goodness, Jude, you are still here! I feared we had missed you! John has had a change of heart and wants you to return with us to the cave." I took a deep breath to collect myself,

"May I ask what changed his mind?" I enquired. Prochurus answered,

"He prayed all night and was guided to come down here this morning to preach. He thought you would come to listen. When he saw the look in your face as he preached, he realized he had allowed his emotions to blur his judgement. He had acted in haste, and not from his heart. Please, come with me, now - John is keen to see you."

As Prochurus and I made our way up the hill, he turned to me and said,

"John has never talked about these events, so I cannot comment. It was courageous of you to come and visit John here, and I respect you for that. Whatever he did, he has more than atoned for his deeds, serving our Lord for over 50 years!"

I said nothing. Prochurus went on,

"I can see you are well intentioned - an honest young man with a pure heart and a sharp mind - I will do anything I can to help bridge this feud between your families... John is stubborn, increasingly as he gets older!"

As we approached the cave, I could see John sat on the same rock we had sat on the previous day, waiting for us. As I came close, he smiled and beckoned for me to sit next to him. He put his hand on my shoulder,

"I apologise for sending you away yesterday. You were right - it is nothing to do with you. I always blamed your grandmother Mary Magdalene for the death of my brother James. I do not wish to discuss it any further, but I have had much time for introspection over the years, particularly here on Patmos, and I can now see she was not directly responsible. You are indeed a promising servant of our Lord and I wish to encourage that. It is time to move forward. I do not intend to take my grievances to the grave with me."

Prochurus appeared from the cave with bread and water which we took together as we prayed. John went inside and reappeared with some notes which he silently handed to me. I had earned his trust. I in turn handed him my copy of *The Shepherd of Hermas* which I had written in Rome.

Prochorus laid out some animal skins inside the cave and motioned for us to retire. I peered inside and saw the shallow cave was only around 12 feet deep. John settled down, laying his head on a smooth rock which served as a pillow. Above him was a niche in the rock wall which he used to raise himself up. Above the niche was a wooden cross which John had carved himself.

I was wide awake and so read John's notes from cover to cover by candlelight. It was beatific prose, the words truly spoke to my heart and my whole body resonated with joy.

When I awoke the next morning, John and Prochorus were outside warming their hands around a fire. It was still cool in the early mornings. John greeted me warmly and said to me,

"I enjoyed reading your book. I liked the way you blended your own experiences and use of allegory to get the message of Christ across. It will appeal to both newcomers to the faith and those further down the spiritual path. I can see why you were instructed to share it with the presbyters in Rome." I smiled, although I was jumping for joy inside - this was high praise indeed. I in turn complimented him on *Revelation*.

Over the next few days I had wonderful discussions with John and Prochorus - I revelled in this theological debate. I asked a thousand questions - mainly about his time with Yeshua - he was the only surviving apostle from the original twelve. But he had so many stories from his fifty years of teaching. I felt so privileged and enriched from listening to them both.

I was reluctant to leave, but I also did not want to overstay my welcome.

John asked where I was heading for, and I said I had no plans. He suggested I visit Ignatius, who had been one of his most promising disciples in Ephesus and was now bishop of Antioch. John went onto say that when Ignatius was a 20 year old new disciple he had written to Mother Mary when she was staying in the house that John built for her outside Ephesus from 55 - 56. Even to this day he could recite Ignatius' letter - Mother Mary had been so moved by his words that she had shown it to John.

"To Mary the Christ-bearer, her Ignatius. You ought to strengthen and console me, a neophyte* and new disciple of John, from whom I have learned many things about Yeshua, things wondrous to tell, and I am dumbfounded at hearing them.

My heart's desire is to be assured about these things that I have heard, as you were always so close to Yeshua and he shared his secrets with you. Fare you well, and let the neophytes who are with me be strengthened in the faith, by you, through you, and in you." Mother Mary answered him as follows,

"To my beloved fellow disciple Ignatius, this humble handmaid of Yeshua. The things you have heard and learned from John are true. Believe in them, hold on to them, be steadfast in carrying out your Christian commitment and shape your life and conduct on it.

I will come to you with John, to visit you, and those who are with you. Stand firm and do manfully in the faith. Do not let the hardships of persecution shake you, and may your spirit be strong and joyful in your salvation. Amen". John then asked Prochurus to fetch him a scroll of papyri and stylus,

"Jude, you remind me of Ignatius with your quick mind, passion and steadfastness. I will send you with a letter of introduction - you will gain much from spending time with Ignatius."

Of course, Clement had been right after all. My mind was still playing tricks with me, allowing doubts to creep in.

There was still healing to be done, but the chasm between John and our family had narrowed greatly. The process had started and

* Neophyte : a new convert to religion

hopefully would continue.

Before I left, I found myself kneeling at John's feet, asking him to bless me on my journey.

In such a short time, I found myself loving and respecting this remarkable man.

Chapter III

Bishop Ignatius of Antioch

June 86 Antioch, Syria

I took a boat to Salamis, Cyprus and then onto Seleucia, the seaport of Antioch*. On the ship from Cyprus to Seleucia, I met a friendly Antiochene called Philip, who filled me in on the history of his native city.

Seleucia was some four miles to the north of the River Orontes estuary, nestling between small rivers on the western slopes of the Coryphaeus, one of the southern summits of the Amenus mountains. After the rocky island of Patmos, the view of the coastline and surrounding mountains took my breath away.

There was an outer and an inner harbour; as our ship entered the inner one the Mediterranean swell was reduced to a glassy calm. We barely nudged the quay as we came alongside and three crew members leapt ashore to secure the mooring lines. Philip pointed me in the direction of Antioch, which lay some 17 miles to the east, following the course of the River Orontes. Its deep and rapid waters wound round the bases of high and precipitous cliffs, or by richly cultivated banks, where the vine and the fig tree, the myrtle, the bay, the ilex, and the arbutus tree mingled with dwarf oak and sycamore.

Antioch was an ancient Greek city, situated at the junction of two mountain chains, where the River Orontes broke through to the fertile Antioch plain, a level area five miles wide and ten miles in length. The river brought down timber, fish and vegetable produce from a lake, about a mile upstream from the city.

Antioch was placed on a bend of the river; partly on an island, partly on an embankment which formed the left bank, and partly on the steep and craggy ascent of Mount Silpios, which rose abruptly to the south.

Antioch was founded near the end of the fourth century BC by

*Antioch's ruins lie near the city of Antakya, Turkey.

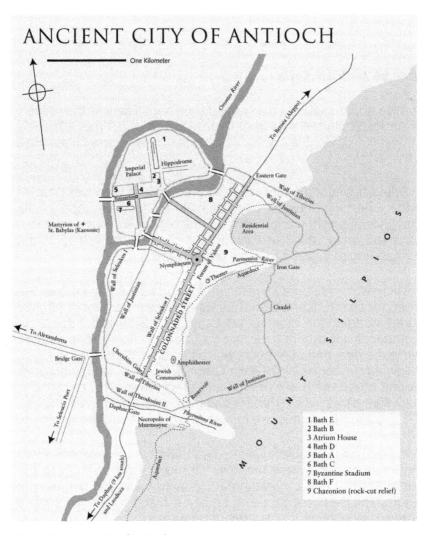

ANCIENT CITY OF ANTIOCH

One Kilometer

Orontes River

To Beroea (Aleppo)

1

Imperial Palace

Hippodrome

2
3

Eastern Gate

5
4

Wall of Tiberius

Ceramicus

Wall of Justinian

6
7

8

Martyrion of +
St. Babylas (Kaoussie)

Residential Area

Wall of Seleucus I

Nymphaeum

Forum of Valens

9

Parmenios River

Iron Gate

Theater

Aqueduct

Wall of Justinian

Citadel

To Alexandretta

Wall of Seleucus I

COLONNADED STREET

Bridge Gate

Cherubim Gate

Amphitheater

Wall of Tiberius

Jewish Community

Wall of Theodosius II

Reservoir

Wall of Justinian

To Seleucia Port

Daphne Gate

Necropolis of Mnemosyne

Phyrminus River

MOUNT SILPIOS

To Daphne (9 km south) and Laodicea

Aqueduct

1 Bath E
2 Bath B
3 Atrium House
4 Bath D
5 Bath A
6 Bath C
7 Byzantine Stadium
8 Bath F
9 Charonion (rock-cut relief)

Figure 2: Ancient city of Antioch

Seleucus I Nictator, one of Alexander the Great's generals. The site was reputedly chosen through ritual means. An eagle, the bird of Zeus, had been given a piece of sacrificial meat and the city was founded on the site to which the eagle carried the offering.

Antioch grew under the successive Seleucid kings until it became a city of remarkable beauty. Its geographical, military and economic position resulted in it rivalling Alexandria as the chief city of the Near East. The city was the capital of the Seleucid Empire until 63 BC, when the Romans took control, making it the seat of the Roman governor.

After Rome and Alexandria, Antioch was the third most important city in the Roman Empire. It covered almost 4.5 square miles within the walls of which one quarter was mountain.

The new city was populated by a mix of local settlers that Athenians brought from the nearby city of Antigonia, Macedonia, and Jews, who unlike the Alexandrian Jews, were given full status from the beginning. The population of the city peaked to 500,000 people during the early Roman period.

The original city of Seleucus was laid out by the architect Xenarius in imitation of the grid plan of Alexandria. Two great colonnaded streets intersected in the centre. Shortly afterwards a second quarter was laid out on the east side, enclosed with a wall of its own. In the Orontes, north of the city, lay a large island which became a third walled city. A fourth and last quarter was added by Antiochus IV Epiphanes, which gave its name to a residential district. Hence Antioch was known as a *tetrapolis*.

Fine houses went up; the first closed drains and private piped water systems were installed. Public spaces were landscaped. Not only watermills but also aqueducts were built. Schools were founded, and the arts and sciences - geometry, astronomy, philosophy, rhetoric, oratory and drama - were rigorously studied. A system of Greek law was established.

Due to its impressive appearance, the city of Antioch earned the epiphet "Golden", but the city needed constant restoration due to the regular earthquakes which occurred there. An earthquake that shook Antioch in 37 caused the emperor Caligula to send two senators to report on the condition of the city. Another quake caused significant damage in the subsequent reign of Emperor Claudius.

I crossed the River Orontes and entered the city through the Bridge Gate. The simple street grid system reminded me of my home town, Alexandria, and made it easy for me to navigate my way to the Jewish quarter, which I entered through the Cherubim Gate. Titus had captured the Cherubim from the Jewish temple, when Jerusalem was besieged and captured in 70.

I made my way to the synagogue and asked where I would find Bishop Ignatius. I was met with smiling faces, happy to oblige - he was clearly popular with the local Jewish population. A young boy of ten or so was told to accompany me through the maze of narrow streets to his lodgings, where Ignatius lived with his housekeeper. I knocked at the door and handed my letter of introduction to the housekeeper. She quickly scurried into the back to find the bishop. He appeared without delay, looking so pleased to see me, greeting me like an old friend.

Dressed in a simple brown tunic, he was of middle age, his wispy hair and beard already grey. He was sprightly, energetic and looked at me with kind, inquisitive grey eyes.

Without hesitation, Ignatius invited me into his home and made me welcome. I felt he would have done so letter or no letter - he had a special aura about him. Remarkable, and yet unassuming.

Ignatius said his housekeeper, Apphia would prepare us a light meal, but first she would show me to my room where I could refresh myself. Water was so abundant in this city, not only the public baths, but every house had its own fountain. I had been travelling three days and nights since I left Patmos, and was most grateful when Apphia appeared at the door with a bowl of warm water and a cotton drying cloth - I freshened up before hurrying to re-join Ignatius.

I am careful who I share my family history with, but felt I could be open with Ignatius. In his humble way, Ignatius said he felt greatly honoured to have the grandson of Mary Magdalene and Yeshua stay with him for however long I wished.

I told him everything; why I had had to leave Alexandria, my spiritual crisis, my extraordinary time with Clement and the visions which had led me to writing *The Shepherd of Hermas*, and most recently, my time with John in Patmos.

Ignatius listened intently; he looked unfazed by my errant life in Alexandria, and very interested in my experiences with Clement and John. He was delighted to hear John was well and thriving. Ignatius said,

"You have already been blessed by two great guides from the divine, I humbly follow in their footsteps. It seems your spiritual crisis has passed, but I am happy to share my own experiences, both as a disciple of John and Bishop of Antioch. I am going to give you a short history of how Christianity has evolved here in Antioch, as it will help you to understand the present situation in Antioch." He continued,

"The Christian Church was formed and found on Pentecost in Jerusalem. In 35, as the apostles dispersed, Peter, Paul and Barnabus travelled to Syria forming communities at Antioch and Tyre. They spent a year in the area, dividing their time between the two communities, teaching large numbers. With their nascent Christian community they founded and built a Cave Church, carved into the mountainside on Mount Staurin near the city of Antioch." Ignatius suddenly stopped and said,

"I am not going to describe our little church - I would like you to see it with your own eyes. But this will have to wait until the morning."

I was weary from my journey and happy to retire early. I had not slept in a bed since I left Pope Clement in Rome and remembered little after laying my head down. I left my curtains ajar so I would awake with sunrise; dawn seemed to arrive moments later. A feeling of excitement surged through my body when I recounted my whereabouts. I quickly dressed to join Ignatius downstairs.

Ignatius was sat at his desk writing and said without looking up,

"I read *The Shepherd of Hermas* last night - powerful words young man. You clearly have a gift and should continue. But you must be famished - let us eat - Apphia has laid out a light breakfast in the garden."

We sat in the courtyard and I devoured home-made bread, tomatoes, olives and feta cheese, washed down with cool spring water.

Ignatius ate little and went inside to take a large key out of the top drawer of his desk. He held up the key and announced,

"Here is the key to our jewel in the mountainside! Are you ready?" I jumped to my feet as he shouted to Apphia that we were going out for a few hours. Off we went, striding through the streets of the Jewish quarter towards the double colonnaded main street.

Ignatius said the number and splendour of public buildings was great, as the Seleucid kings and queens had vied with each other in embellishing their city. But it received still further embellishment from a series of Roman emperors. In 64 BC, Syria was reduced to a province and Pompey gave Antioch the privilege of autonomy. He would gladly show me the city at another time, but for now his mind was set on the cave church.

As we came to the end of the main street, we exited the city through the Eastern gate and made our way eastwards along the Wall of Tiberius towards the foothills of Mount Staurin. Leaving the gardens and olive groves behind, we began to climb steeply and the vegetation was reduced to scrub, rock and spindly trees.

I paused to catch my breath and gaze at Mount Staurin looming above us. I turned around to admire the view of Antioch; the river was easy to spot, forming an island where the magnificent Imperial Palace was located, connected to the city by five bridges, and commanding a view of the open country to the west. Ignatius pointed out the hippodrome and public baths which were also located on this island.

I could also see the double colonnaded street which we had just traversed and ran from east to west for a length of four miles; other streets crossed it at right angles, to the river on the west side, and the groves and gardens of the hill on the east side. At the intersection of the main street was the Nymphaeum, an impressive water fountain.

The Cave church was just over a mile from the Eastern Gate - it was a steep climb and we walked in silence. Ignatius turned off to the right and the ground levelled off as we found ourselves at the foot of a cliff face. And there it was - the Church of St Peter. I stood in awe, rooted to the spot, and marvelled at how Peter, Paul and Barnabus, together with their followers, had filled in the cave entrance with rocks, painstakingly chiselled to the right shape by hand. A labour of love... Stone steps led up to an entrance through a large dark blue wooden door. There were three windows above to allow light in.

Ignatius took the key out of his pocket and unlocked the door. Sunlight poured in and as my eyes adjusted, I could see the cave was a depth of 40 feet or so, with a width of 30 feet and a height of 20 feet. It was incredible! It was as if it had been designed by our Lord himself for his faithful followers to assemble in safety, away from unfriendly eyes.

There were wooden pews running along each side and a stone altar and chair near the back of the cave. A wooden stand was off to the left side where Ignatius read the lesson. His followers wanted to build a pulpit for him to climb up to and preach from, but Ignatius said he wanted to be at eye level with his congregation - as we are all equal in the eyes of God.

Ignatius made his way to the back corner of the church and lifted

Figure 3: Cave Church of St Peter, Antioch

up a well- worn rush mat. Underneath was a wooden board covering a tunnel entrance. They had taken the precaution of installing an escape route which opened to the mountainside in case of sudden raids and attacks!

Ignatius pointed to where water seeped in from the rocks above onto the cave floor. It was collected in earthenware bowls - Ignatius scooped a handful to his lips and motioned for me to do the same. It was straight from the mountain, ice cool and delicious.

It was used for baptisms and ministered to the sick as blessed water, with many testifying to its healing properties.

Peter and Paul were considered the co-founders of the Patriarchate of Antioch, with Peter becoming the first Bishop in 45. The Cave Church was named after him - the Church of Peter. When Peter moved to Rome in 53, he was succeeded by Evodius who was the church leader until 70, when Ignatius succeeded him as Bishop. After Peter's martyrdom, the Cave Church was known as the Church of St Peter.

Ignatius said that followers of Yeshua were first known as *Christians*, here in Antioch. Originally known as 'Followers of the Way of the Heart', this was abbreviated to 'Followers of the Way' and then *Christians*. Citizens of Antioch were renowned for their wit, ridicule and affinity for nicknames, so it is no surprise the term 'Christian' was coined here.

As Jewish Christianity originated at Jerusalem, so Gentile Christianity started at Antioch, then the leading centre of the Hellenistic East, with Peter and Paul as its apostles. Christians who were scattered from Jerusalem because of persecution, fled to Antioch. They were joined by Christians from Cyprus and Cyrene who migrated to Antioch.

It was a cosmopolitan community and Antioch was considered the cradle of the Church. From Antioch it spread to the various cities and provinces of Syria, among the Hellenistic Syrians and Jews who, as a result of the great rebellion against the Romans in 70, were driven out from Jerusalem and Palestine into Syria.

After the end of the war, Jews across the Syrian province suffered reprisals from the Roman victors. Jewish captives were showcased at various events, and the Romans undertook other degrading actions; outside Antioch the Roman general Titus set up winged bronze figures from the temple, and a theatre was built from the spoils of the temple on the site of a synagogue. The emperor Vespasian imposed a Jewish temple tax and used it to rebuild the Temple of Jupiter in Rome.

These humiliating actions were not restricted to the Jews - it was the normal way Romans treated conquered peoples. When the non-Jewish population of Antioch petitioned Titus to drive the Jews out of the city, or at least strip them of their rights, the general departed and left the status of the Jews unchanged. Riots and civic unrest were not in the interest of Rome. But the fact the Roman authorities protected the Jews from open attacks from the non-Jewish population caused further resentment.

The fusion of Roman, Greek and Jewish elements stood Antioch in good stead for the part it played in the development of early Christianity.

However, this 'melting pot' of ethnicities resulted in cultural tensions within the early Christian movement between the Hellenized Jews and Greek-speaking Judeo- Christians centred around Antioch and Syrian 'Diasporas', and the Aramaic speaking Jewish converts to Christianity based in Jerusalem and neighbouring Israeli towns.

Peter and Paul had been engaged in a theological standoff. Paul publicly opposed Peter for eating with Gentiles, and then separating from them to appease a Jewish-Christian party from Jerusalem. This raised important questions; was it necessary to observe the dietary practices of the Torah in order to be a Christian? Could Jewish Christians eat the same foods or eat at the same table with Gentile Christians?

These social tensions were eventually surmounted by the emergence of a new, typically Antiochian Greek doctrine spearheaded by Paul (himself a Hellenized Cilician Jew), which practised a more 'liberal' form of Judaism. Paul proposed that everyone could eat at the same table. Peter was more flexible. He followed Jewish regulations when eating with Jews and then abandoned such regulations when eating with Jews in mixed company.

Ignatius paused and said,

"For me there is neither Jew nor Greek; there is neither slave nor free; there is neither male nor female. For we are all one in Christ."

Ignatius then baptized me at the altar and we sat down together on one of the pews and prayed; for how long I could not say, as when I am in this space I am outside time. A prayer of thanksgiving for all the blessings I was showered with on a daily basis, for guidance, humility, patience and wisdom. I felt humbled by the efforts and achievements of the apostles - to build this beautiful little church for the Christian community.

I had so many questions for this sage man, but felt I should be patient and wait for him to decide what to share with me. Ignatius must have read my mind - he turned and looked at me and said,

"I see you have many questions for me, young man. For now I will say this. *Take care to do all things in harmony with God, with the bishop presiding in the place of God, and with the presbyters in the place of the council of the apostles, and with the deacons, who are most dear to me, entrusted with the business of Christ, who was with the Father from the beginning and is at last made manifest."**

Ignatius modelled his own writing after Paul, Peter and John, and quoted Paul freely in his letter to the Ephesians,

"*Let my spirit be counted as nothing for the sake of the cross, which is a stumbling block to those that do not believe, but to us*

*Letter to the Magnesians 2, 6:1

salvation and eternal life." Ignatius continued,

"There will be many churches built within your lifetime, and it is important they remember we are all part of the whole; *Catholic* comes from the Greek word *katholikos - according to the whole.* We are all One..." Ignatius put his arm on my shoulder and said,

"You are welcome to stay with me as long as you wish. I sense you have ideas of your own which I would be most interested in hearing - you are here for a reason and I am sure I will learn something!" The humility of this man was an inspiration to me.

I was pleasantly surprised when Ignatius appointed me as his deputy - I did not feel qualified and was unsure how long I was staying. Ignatius clearly had more foresight than me.

Just as I had done in Rome, he wanted me to share the teachings in *The Shepherd of Hermas* with the church officers not only in Antioch, but also in other cities and provinces of Syria, as the number of Christians was growing daily.

I accompanied him on all his church duties, but sometimes I went alone if there were specific queries with my book. Ignatius had appointed Bishops in the other cities, who in turn chose their own deacons and presbyters for the smooth running of their churches. Ignatius was always available to offer advice, or at other times, just listen. He used to say,

"We have two ears and one mouth for a reason, Jude!"

Ignatius replaced the Sabbath with the Lord's Day, celebrated on a Sunday.

Two issues which concerned Ignatius were the Judaizing heresy and Docetism*. He warned the Magnesians against living according to Judaism and said,

"It is monstrous to talk of Christ and to practice Judaism". The

*Docetism: the belief that Yeshua's body was not human but of celestial matter, and so his sufferings were only apparent.

Philadephians were also warned about Judaism,

"Be not seduced by strange doctrines nor by antiquated fables, which are profitless. For if even unto this day we live after the manner of Judaism, we avow that we have not received grace... If then those who had walked in ancient practices attained unto newness of hope, no longer observing Sabbaths but fashioning their lives after the Lord's day, on which our life also arose through Him... how shall we be able to live apart from Him?" *

The members at Tralles and at Smyrna were asked to consider the evil results of Docetism. Yeshua was truly in the flesh. He rose in the flesh. To reject this was to deny him completely.

Ignatius stressed the value of the Eucharist, calling it a "medicine of immortality". He regarded salvation as one being free from the powerful fear of death and to bravely face martyrdom.

Ignatius had heard angels standing on a mountain singing antiphons**. He took this as a sign and introduced the practice of singing Psalms in Church.

He emphasised the importance of the unity of the church and its patient endurance in its service of Christ. Ignatius put a high value on celibacy although it was not compulsory.

He was emphatic that Christ was God, God who had become a man. Christ was born from a virgin, was baptized, suffered and rose again. He was the son of David and the Son of God.

Ignatius considered the government of the Church of extreme importance. The bishop was like God or Christ, the elders were compared to the apostles. The deacons were the servants of the Church, deacons of the mysteries of Christ. The elders were attuned to the bishop as the strings of the harp. Ignatius had introduced the custom of there being a single bishop in each church and advocated this as universal church procedure.

*Ignatius to the Magnesians 8:1
** Antiphon - a sung chant

Bishop Polycarp of Smyrna

Ignatius said he had invited his great friend and fellow disciple of John, Bishop Polycarp of Smyrna to visit us. They had met when Polycarp had joined John in 76; Polycarp was just 21 years old and Ignatius took Polycarp under his wing.

Ignatius was quickly impressed with Polycarp; not only did he have a sharp mind, he had self discipline, and was even tempered at all times. He developed an unshakeable belief in the Word of our Lord, which he conveyed with gravity, love and great countenance. He spoke of conversations he had had with John and many others who had seen and been with Yeshua, words he had heard directly from their mouths.

John was also impressed with Polycarp - he rose quickly through the ranks and became one of the youngest bishops to be appointed by John. He was still in his twenties when he became Bishop of Smyrna. I was feeling a little nervous about meeting Polycarp, but I need not have been. Although small and wiry in stature, his deportment and presence suggested otherwise. I was struck by the light in his face, accentuated by a broad smile which was there continually.

Ignatius had answered the door knowing who the visitor would be, and I smiled as I watched the two men embrace one another warmly - clearly there was great affection and respect between them. After laughter and hearty slaps on each other's backs, Ignatius introduced me as his young itinerant disciple. Polycarp turned to me and said,

"Jude, what a pleasure and an honour to meet you - Ignatius has spoken of little else in his letters to me since your arrival - I fear I have been replaced!" The two men broke into raucous laughter, so happy to be in one another's company.

Polycarp stayed for ten days and we talked long into the night, every night... His ideas were not dissimilar to Ignatius, but Polycarp was more tolerant. Not all were blessed with the gifts of belief, devotion, gratitude and appreciation - it was not an easy road being a Christian in these times, and followers should be treated as errant children or straying sheep - not sinful. I felt incredibly blessed to have had the opportunity to meet and spend time with four of Christ's servants; Pope Clement, John, Ignatius and Polycarp.

My faith had grown steadily, slowly but surely, and the inner torment and doubts had been silenced, for now anyway.

I was neither looking for, or prepared for, what happened next.

Chapter IX

Helena

July 86 Antioch, Syria

She was called Helena, a beautiful Greek Jewish woman born in Jerusalem, but ousted with her family in the Roman siege of the city in 70. She later told me she was just four years old when her parents had fled from Jerusalem. She had few memories of Jerusalem, but remembered her family leaving in a hurry in an atmosphere of fear and controlled panic.

I noticed her instantly in church because of her wavy blonde hair and piercing blue eyes. She attended the weekly Sunday service in the Cave Church of St Peter with her mother, Ruth. She walked with her head held high, in a graceful unhurried fashion. She had an air of calm and serenity about her which I found captivating.

The first time I caught her eye in church, I felt a bolt of excitement surge through my entire body, and, much to my embarrassment, I blushed. I stared at my sandals, breathing deeply to collect myself. Fortunately, it was dark in the church and I hoped it had gone unnoticed. But on the way back to our lodgings, Ignatius said,

"Ah, I see love is in the air...!" I stopped and wheeled around,

"What do you mean?" I retorted, trying to sound calm.

"I saw the way Helena eyed you and the reaction it had in you... She is a beautiful woman, do not deny or be embarrassed by your feelings."

"But I have not even spoken to her!" I protested!

"You did not have to - your soul knows and your body too. Just your mind is a little confused."

"What do you advise me to do Ignatius? I have no money, no

prospects, not even a roof over my head - why would she be interested in me?"

"Well she clearly is, and she is from a wealthy family - her father Aaron is a successful timber merchant. You were not put on this earth to make money, our Lord has a greater purpose in mind for you - he will provide for both of you if it is meant to be".

I lay in bed that night, sleeping fitfully. I dreamt of Helena of course - I awoke covered in sweat and an undeniable longing in my heart, and stirring in my loins.

It seemed like an age until the following Sunday when I could see Helena again. After the end of the service, I stood behind Ignatius at the door, as he bade farewell to each member of his congregation. When Helena came with her mother Ruth, Ignatius introduced me to them both. He said he did not know how long I would be staying with him, and so he would be most grateful if they could show me around the city, as he had been too busy to do so. Helena cast her eyes down as Ruth said they would be delighted to oblige. My heart leapt inside with delight. And what a wily old match-maker Ignatius was.

The following morning my tour guides, Ruth and Helena, appeared at Ignatius's door. As Helena was a single young woman of 20 years, Ruth would accompany us as chaperone - I may have had an introduction from a bishop, but she would make her own mind up as to who would keep company with her precious only daughter.

Ruth did all the talking. She said the character of the local inhabitants was affected by the climate - luxurious and effeminate. A high Greek civilization mixed with Oriental elements, and particularly superstitions of early Babylonian or Chaldaean astrology.

About five miles south west of the city lay the paradise of Daphne*, a park of woods and waters. Its central feature was a great temple to the Pythian Apollo, founded by Seleucus I, enriched with a cult statue of the god, as Musagetes, the Leader of the Muses.

*Daphne was a Naiad nymph in Greek mythology, a minor goddess associated with fountains, wells and springs.

A sanctuary of the Greek goddess Hecate was constructed underground - she was worshipped as a protective goddess who bestowed prosperity and daily blessings on the family.

The beauty and lax morals of Daphne were celebrated all over the western world and it enjoyed a reputation for being a populous resort, full of the most erudite men and rich in the most liberal studies. As it was some way out of the city, we did not make it there on this occasion.

We made our way along the colonnaded street to the impressive Nymphaeum, which we could see from over a mile away. As we approached, Helena could not contain her excitement - she said she never tired of the grand buildings of her home city. It certainly was impressive.

The Nymphaeum was consecrated to the nymphs, and as it was located above a tributary of the Orontes, was a natural grotto and supplied water to a large marble fountain.

The monument was in the form of a rotunda built around the fountain; water cascaded through seven carved lions' heads into small basins on the circular side walk. The rotunda was adorned with statues and paintings, protected from the elements by a half-dome roof. The Nymphaeum served the threefold purpose of a sanctuary, reservoir and assembly room. It was also a popular venue for marriage celebrations.

We left the Nymphaeum behind us and headed west towards the island, where we crossed one of the five bridges. The Imperial palace and the Hippodrome dominated the skyline. I had grown up in Alexandria and so was accustomed to impressive palaces built under the Ptolemies; each successive King had added a new residence increasing the palace area to a third of the city. But nothing prepared me for the size and scale of the Hippodrome.

One of the most famous sites of Antioch, built by the Romans under Augustus, first emperor of the Roman Empire, when the city had more than half a million inhabitants, was the Circus of Antioch.

It was a Roman hippodrome, mainly used for chariot racing. Modelled on the Circus Maximus in Rome, it measured more than 1,610 feet and 98 feet wide with a capacity of up to 80,000 spectators.

Chariot racing was a much more popular spectator sport than gladiatoring, but equally perilous for the participants. The two wheeled open chariot provided no protection for the driver, and inevitable clashes resulted in serious injury or death. This added to the entertainment for the blood thirsty crowds.

As we overlooked the arena, I could visualise the horse driven chariots careering around the track at breakneck speed by daring young men, usually slaves, racing for their lives, cheered on by the roar of 80,000 people.

The love of frivolous amusements became a passion in the contests of the Hippodrome. On many occasions, the violent feelings of the people broke out and blood was spilled in the stands, as well as by the contestants.

There were seven bath houses on the island; sex and class determined which one you were able to use.

We sat down on a grassy area under a tree to take shade from the midday sun. Ruth eyed me cautiously and asked me why I had come to Antioch. I realized this was an interview, and it was important for me to make a good impression. But my heart told me to tell her the whole story, although I glossed over my exploits in Alexandria, and the reason for my sudden departure from the city.

When I had finished she sat there quietly for some time; I looked at Helena and she smiled at me, a smile of encouragement. It was so wonderful to be in her company, to be close enough to smell her scent - her luxurious, shiny hair and smooth olive skin glistening in the sun.

I was interested in what Ruth had been saying, but seriously distracted by Helena's presence - I felt almost bewitched. Eventually Ruth said,

"I have no reason to disbelieve you, but I need some time to take in what you have just told me - if you are the only male heir of Yeshua, it has serious implications for whoever you choose to marry." I could not disagree. Ruth was no fool; it was not difficult to see I had feelings for her precious, only daughter - few would consider me an ideal suitor.

I was escorted back to my lodgings and Ruth asked to see Ignatius. He never told me what he said, but it must have been favourable, as I was now allowed to go for day time walks with Helena without a chaperone!

We saw each other almost every day, and we talked endlessly and effortlessly. Even though she was from a wealthy family, she was understated and dressed with simplicity and taste, in every shade of blue from powder to indigo, in materials soft and luxurious to the touch. The only jewellery she wore was a copper bracelet which glowed with burnished beauty through years of wear.

Her candour and basic honesty enabled me in turn to be candid with her, and I told her all about my wanton days in Alexandria. I poured my heart out to her. I felt this woman could replenish my store of hope, no matter what, and save me from feeling defeated by the world, infusing me with her own brave, dauntless example. Her feet were firmly planted on terra firma - she was both predictable and dependable. This was the first thing I had ever been certain of in my life, I had absolutely no doubt that she was the one for me.

I prayed that Helena would consider me good enough for her and say yes... I wrote to Sarah to tell her about my intention to marry Helena. Even though my mother had not met Helena, I knew what her answer would be, she had married for love and been happily married for 30 years - she would wish the same for me.

I am not certain if it was as a result of spending time with Clement, John, Ignatius and Polycarp, or being in love, or both, but I felt a desire to write. I had not written since my time in Rome. Once I started, I could not stop. I would awake in the early morning with ideas, rise at first light and write until dusk, unless I was accompanying Ignatius on church duties, or meeting Helena. I would call on her late morning, and we would walk all over the city and beyond - regularly visiting Daphne park with its romantic lake, statues and woodland. This was where I proposed to her - she accepted, and we celebrated with our first kiss. I could feel energy surging through every cell in my body. I had never felt so alive in my entire life and I could not remember ever feeling so happy.

I carried on the family tradition started by Mary Magdalene and then my mother Sarah, in writing either under a pseudonym or anonymously. I wrote *The Paraphrase of Shem* and *The Didache**, or *The Teaching of the Twelve Apostles.*

I felt my experience of staying on Patmos with John, hearing about and reading *Revelation*, inspired me to write *The Paraphrase of Shem*, an allegorical writing relating the ascension and recension to Earth of Shem, son of Noah. Shem is given a revelation from a being called *Derdekas* (son of Infinite Light). It recounts a version of the Biblical Flood, Sodom's destruction, and the baptism and resurrection of the Saviour. The text first describes three powers: Light, Spirit and Darkness. The Light is a dominant power of reason, and the Darkness a malevolent power of chaos. The meek power of Spirit stands between them.

Derdekas is a gnostic Saviour aiming to spread salvation and combat the evils plaguing earth. He descends into the world in disguise in order to save the Spirit from the Darkness and in so doing, provides the world with more of the knowledge and deliverance connected to the Light.

It refers to Shem as the 'first person on Earth', which depending on the reader's interpretation can also be connected to Yeshua who said,

---

* The Didache was discovered in 1873 by Philotheos Bryennios, Metropolitan of Nicodemia, in the Codex Hierosolymitanus

"Before Abraham was, I AM".

After the male monastic Essene community at Qumran* dispersed in 68, twelve members came to join our community at Lake Mareotis. They brought with them a copy of their 'Code of Conduct', which Sarah read with great interest. Over time, many of their ways were incorporated into our daily life at Lake Mareotis.

I had also studied the 'Code of Conduct', which inspired me to write *The Didache*. It is a manual about how to provide leadership to a congregation: a summary of my findings from talking to Pope Clement, John, Bishop Ignatius and Bishop Polycarp, on policies and practices for leaders of churches. It presented a code of conduct, a list of practices, and an explanation of common customs. *The Didache* gave advice on how to adapt Jewish Christian practices for Gentile Christians. We had to be inclusive.

On 1st September 86, just six weeks after our first chaperoned date, Ignatius married us in a simple ceremony in the Cave Church of St Peter. I had loved this church from the moment I had entered it for the first time - little did I know I would be getting married in it within two months. The guest list was limited by the church capacity - Helena's parents had lots of friends, but we restricted it to her immediate family, and members of the congregation who had welcomed me into their Christian community.

The service was followed by a reception at Helena's parents' house. This was not our idea, but we did not wish to offend Helena's family, who had welcomed me into their family. We filed down from the church to their house in the Charonion, a wealthy residential area in the north east of the city. The houses were sumptuous with substantial gardens - it was a lavish party with no expense spared.

It helped that her parents were Christians, but clearly some of their friends were somewhat puzzled by the match - I was an unremarkable foreigner without a shekel to my name. I had asked Helena's family to be discrete about my lineage - it would not be beyond the Romans to put a bounty on my head... I was not an advocate of martyrdom - I was young and had things to do.

* Qumran is located in the West Bank, Israel and was discovered by archaeologists in the 19th century. It became famous after the discovery of the Dead Sea Scrolls in 1947.

In the short time I had been in Antioch, with introductions from Ignatius, I had secured some cabinet making work. In addition, Ignatius was paying me a small stipend which enabled us to rent a place of our own - simple, but we were just happy to be living together as man and wife.

I built a wooden lean-to at the rear so I would not need to rent an additional workshop. This was home, for now - Helena understood that we were destined to return to Lake Mareotis to help run the community sometime in the future. Neither of us was in a rush to do so - my writing was going well and we would not be able to co-habit at Lake Mareotis, as it did not accommodate married couples.

We were so happy in our first year of marriage - I was busy writing and cabinet making for wealthy *Antiochenes*, and Helena had become an invaluable administrative assistant to Ignatius.

In December, just three months after our wedding, Helena said she had something important to tell me. I guessed instantly - she was expecting our first child! Young as we were, at 23 and 20, we were overjoyed at the prospect of becoming parents and keen to share our news with all our family and friends.

Helena went straight to her parents' house to tell her mother, and I excitedly relayed our forthcoming arrival to Ignatius. Ignatius' face lit up when I told him and he said,

"That really is wonderful news Jude, I assume you will be writing to your parents? They will be most eager to meet their new grandchild. As I introduced you, smoothed the passage of your courtship, and then married you, would you please grant me the honour of baptising your first born before returning to Alexandria?"

I froze for a few moments. I had not thought about returning to Alexandria; but of course, Ignatius was right - my parents would be keen to meet their grandchild, the great grandchild of Yeshua and Mary Magdalene, the heir to the blood-line.

I discussed this with Helena, saying that once the baby had been baptized we should plan to return to Lake Mareotis. We could visit her parents every year, and they could come to Lake Mareotis whenever they were able to. We were so in love Helena showed no visible protestation, although I knew in my heart of hearts it would be a big change for her, uprooted from her family and friends.

On 6th June 87, attended by a mid-wife and her mother, Helena gave birth to a baby boy who we named John Julius. John was the first pseudonym my grandmother Mary Magdalene wrote under (*The Secret Book of John* from Codex II).

Julius was the governor of Gaul - he and his wife Domitia had been my family's guardian angels, when Mary Magdalene, Sarah and her inner circle had been shipwrecked and washed up onto the shore in Gaul in 43.

He looked just like his beautiful mother, fair with bright blue eyes. I wrote to Bishop Polycarp to ask him to be our son's godfather (Ignatius had said he was too old and Polycarp was more my age!)

Assisted by Polycarp, Ignatius baptized him when he was two months old. Ruth and Aaron beamed with pride; not only had their daughter produced a son, but there were two bishops at their grandson's baptism!

I was keen to sail to Alexandria before the *euroclydon* season, a cyclonic tempestuous north easterly wind which blows in the Mediterranean in late autumn and winter. We boarded a ship in the port of Seleucia on the 23rd September. John Julius was just three months old.

Helena's family, Ignatius and many members of our church congregation came to bid us farewell. I was sorry to say goodbye to Ignatius, and a few good friends I had made during my stay, but I was going home and looking forward to seeing my family.

It was very different for Helena - she was leaving home for the first time and didn't know when she was going to return. There were no tears, not in public anyway - she considered them a sign of weakness. She didn't like goodbyes either, so she hugged her parents and then scurried onto the ship without looking behind.

All I could do was pray that she would adjust to life in our community at Lake Mareotis.

Chapter V

The Essenes, Lake Mareotis

Out of cloud covered history came the Essenes. They were known as the 'Mysterious or Secret Ones', the 'Silent Ones', 'People of Hidden Strength', the 'Modest Ones' and the 'Holy Men'. Their ethics and morals were respected above all people. Their word was their bond. They ascribed all things to God. They were frugal, virtuous, believed in immortality and spiritual evolution through an individual's conscious and unconscious efforts.

The Qumran Essene monastic community was formed around 200 BC. The Essenes inexplicably deserted the community around 31 BC, barely leaving a footprint in the desert. They returned in the year 6, increasing their numbers and extending the assembly halls and baptismal pools.

Around 200 years before the birth of Yeshua, the leader of the community, known as the *'Teacher of Righteousness'*, or the 'One', had a vision: an Angel told him that a great Avatar, the Messiah, would come to Earth through the Essenes. But for this to occur, they must follow certain disciplines in order to create a physical body capable of withstanding the powerful vibrations of the Christ Spirit, as well as a group energy powerful enough to open an "energy vortex" or "doorway" into this space-time dimension through which the Christ would enter. The Essene communities were the doorway, Yeshua was the Avatar.

Yeshua grew up with Mary and Joseph at the Mount Carmel family community in Palestine. When he reached 18, he spent a year at Qumran in preparation for his ministry.

The Angels also warned the Essenes of the imminent siege and downfall of Jerusalem which would take place in 70. Everything of value; writings, gold, treasure, was taken out of the city and hidden in the desert.

In 68, the Qumran community once again disbanded. But not before their writings had been safely buried in the surrounding caves for future generations to discover, at a time when they would be safe and humanity was ready to receive them.

Shortly after, when the Roman eagle entered Qumran, it was greeted with hollow silence. The Romans razed everything to the ground. Their members had safely dispersed amongst other communities across Palestine and Egypt. In Palestine they were known as the Essenes, and in Egypt the Therapeutae.

As Mother Mary was an Essene and had moved to Lake Mareotis in 33, the foundation had already been laid for their way of living. As our numbers grew, we also adopted their social organisation

The Essenes were founded by Enoch and according to Pliny, the Roman naturalist, *existed for thousands of ages'*. They were reintroduced by Moses when he came down from Mount Sinai with two tablets of stone;

'Written not with ink, but with the Spirit of the living God; not on tablets of stone, but on tablets of the living heart.'

Moses was the giver of the Law, the One Law.

The Law governs all that takes place in the universe, and all other universes, all activity, all creation, mental or physical. The Law creates life and it creates thought. The sum total of life on all the planets in the universe was termed the *cosmic ocean of life*. And the sum total of currents of thought in the universe was called the *cosmic ocean of thought*. The cosmic ocean of life and cosmic ocean of thought form a dynamic unity of which man is an inseparable part. Every human being is an individualized part of the unity. This unity is the Law, the Eternal Light.

Moses saw the Law broken everywhere. Despite Egypt's great military and political might, there was no law of equality. Misery and slavery existed everywhere; rich and poor alike suffered from oppression, epidemics, and plagues.

Moses observed that ignorance of the Law, of the laws of nature, was responsible for all evils, and that the rulers and the ruled were equally to blame. Moses concluded that everything created as a result of deviation from the Law destroyed itself and in time disappeared. Only the Law was eternal.

Moses wanted his followers to realize they were in constant contact with all forces of life in the visible and invisible universe; and if they contacted these powers consciously, becoming continually conscious of them, they would enjoy perfect health, happiness and harmony in body and mind.

The method of contacting these forces was engraved on the two stone tablets Moses brought down from Mount Sinai, but destroyed when he found the masses were not ready for the teaching. For the masses he gave exoteric teachings in the form of the *Ten Commandments.*

To the few who were ready he taught the method given on the tablets, the *Communion with the Angels.*

The abstract idea of the Law was incorporated into the symbol of a tree, called the *Tree of Life.* It portrayed man as a unit of energy, with thoughts and emotions constantly communing with the totalities of energies in the universe.

The Essenes added to the Tree Angelology - the Science of the Angels. The angels were the forces in the universe. The Essenes petitioned the assistance of these angelic Ones in all aspects of everyday life. They were considered emissaries of the Heavenly Father, residents of the higher planes of life, when called upon, directing their assistance to men of earth in need of their aid.

Yeshua referred to angels at the time of his arrest, when he said,

"Do you think that I cannot ask of my Father, and He will not raise up for me more than twelve legions of angels?

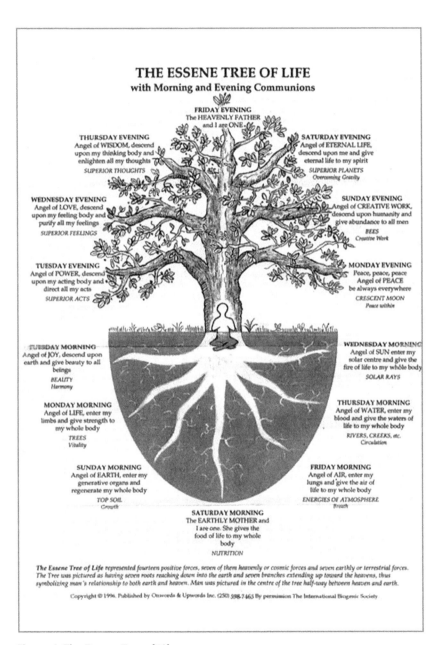

Figure 4: The Essene Tree of Life

The Essenes recognized only the positive and constructive forces in the universe. The Essene Tree of Life represented fourteen positive forces; seven heavenly or cosmic forces and seven earthly forces. The centre branch represents God, the centre root Mother Nature. The roots represented earthly forces and powers; the Earthly Mother, the Angel of Earth, the Angel of Life, the Angel of Joy, the Angel of the Sun, the Angel of Water and the Angel of Air. The seven branches represented cosmic powers; the Heavenly Father and his Angels of Eternal Life, Creative Work, Peace, Power, Love and Wisdom. These were the Essene angels of the visible and invisible worlds.

Man, in the centre of the Tree, was surrounded by the heavenly angels above and the earthly angels below. Contact with the angelic forces was the very essence of their daily life. They knew it took conscious effort to contact them. The Essenes had the deep wisdom to understand that these forces were sources of energy, knowledge and harmony, and to put himself into harmony with the Heavenly Father and Earthly Mother was man's most important activity in life.

They also understood each heavenly force to have an earthly force corresponding to it. These corresponding heavenly and earthly forces were placed on the Essene tree of Life diagonally across from each other, one above and one below man. This made it clear how inseparably we are linked to all the forces, cosmic and terrestrial, and how essential it was to be in perfect harmony with each and every one of the forces and angels.

The Essene might attune himself to the Angel of Water and direct the absorption into his being the cleansing power of water. Attunement to the Angel of Air would provide the life-giving qualities of the atmosphere, while the Angel of Light would furnish the higher spiritual essence it symbolized. Inner association with Angels of Love, Wisdom, Power and others would cause these attributes to be stimulated and strengthened inwardly.

This process was known as *Communion*. The Communions were practised each morning and evening, a different earthly force being meditated upon each morning upon arising, and a different heavenly force each evening before retiring each day of the week. This made a total of fourteen communions during each seven day period.

When Yeshua met with his disciples for the Last Supper, they ate bread as a symbolic Communion with the body, *or energy forces*, and drank wine as a symbolic Communion with his blood, or *spiritual forces*. If this was understood and practiced with conscious awareness, it was a powerful practice for all those who partook in it. A third group of practices was held at noon each day of the week. These were contemplations calling upon the Heavenly Father to send his Angel of Peace to harmonize all areas of a man's life. So important was peace to the Essenes, that they had a special teaching called the *Sevenfold Peace*. They were practised in the following order; Peace with the Body, Peace with the Mind, Peace with the Family, Peace with Humanity, Peace with Culture, Peace with the Earthly Mother and Peace with the Heavenly Father.

The Communions enabled the individual to expand his consciousness and make conscious use of the invisible forces of nature and the cosmos. The Sevenfold Peace was a practical application of this expanded consciousness in everyday life.

The Rite of Baptism existed in three forms; *Initiatory, Personal* and *Baptism by Fire*. Initiatory Baptism was a public ceremony which established contact between the initiate and the superior spheres of life. It is symbolic of purification and a form of rebirth - a moment of supreme spiritual experience.

Personal baptism was practised daily, where the individual reminded himself of the purification essential to spiritual progress and re-established his connection with the invisible planes.

In addition, there was a *Baptism by Fire* - symbolic of a still higher and more spiritual power than Baptism by Water.

There were three main aspects of Essene theology; belief in a Father-Mother God, reincarnation and vegetarianism.

God is a perfect balance of the masculine (Father) and feminine

(Mother) aspects; in the words of Yeshua,

*"God is both male and female, not divided, but the Two in One...
In God the masculine is not without the feminine, nor is the feminine
without the masculine: Love is not without knowledge, Justice is not
without Mercy, the Head is not without the Heart. In God, the
masculine powers and feminine powers are perfectly united as ONE."*

We are each a Divine Child of God, created in the embryonic image
and likeness of the eternal Father-Mother. The essential nature of
God is Oneness. I AM. Masculine causative energy must be balanced
by feminine receptive energy or the individual will be out of balance
and experience pain.

The Essenes were strict vegetarians; their diet was raw fruits,
vegetables, sprouted grains and raw dairy products. They never
touched meat or fermented liquids. They ate their meals in silence,
preceding and ending with prayer.

They knew bodily health had a great deal to do with the receiving
of higher forces, and that a detoxified organism was more adept than
one partially paralyzed by the burden of eliminating bodily poisons
during the hours of sleep.

They were equally careful of their diet in thought and emotions.
They were fully aware that man's subconscious mind is like a
sensitized palate registering everything the individual sees or hears,
and essential to prevent all inferior thoughts, such as fear, anxiety,
insecurity, hatred, ignorance, egotism and intolerance from entering
the subconscious mind.

They understood the natural law that a person cannot think of two
things simultaneously. So, if the mind is filled with positive,
harmonious thoughts, those that are negative and inharmonious
cannot lodge in it. Positive, harmonious thoughts must be
introduced into the subconscious to replace all inferior ones, just as
the cells of the body must be constantly replaced by food, air and
water as the old cells are broken down.

Communions could not be attained through intellectual processes alone, that the force of feelings is also necessary. Feelings can be mastered through discipline. Feelings either create energy or deplete it. By strengthening all the feelings that create energy and avoiding all those that lead to its exhaustion, through perseverance and patient effort. This leads to harmony and a vast storehouse of energy. The feeling that creates the greatest energy is love.

The three enemies of will are dispersion of energy, laziness and sensuality. These can in turn lead to disease. A dynamic, healthy individual commands, and the will obeys; alternatively muscular pain or nervous weakness paralyzes the will. This was one of the reasons the Essenes laid such importance on good health.

They lived a simple life, rising each day before sunrise, to pray and attune to the various angelic forces needed during the day. The inner spiritual atmosphere generated was carried over into all the working activities which followed. They bathed in cold water as a ritual and donned white garments.

Evening was the beginning of their day and their Sabbath began on Friday evening, the first day of their week. This day was given up to study, discussion, the entertaining of visitors and playing musical instruments.

Every seventh Sabbath was called the Great Sabbath and was dedicated to Peace with the Holy Father. This was the transcendental Peace, containing all other aspects of peace.

They spent much time in study of both ancient writings and special branches of learning, such as education and astronomy. They were adept in prophecy for which they prepared by prolonged fasting.

Their way of life enabled them to live to ages of 120 years or more, and they were said to have marvellous strength and endurance. Through their exercise of will they seemed to be above pain. This was frequently tested at the hands of the Romans, who tortured them in an attempt to force them to swear allegiance or eat forbidden food.

Members of the community were from all walks of life. Scholars, wealthy merchants or successful tradesmen all worked for the good of the community. Each had found it impossible to continue practices that offended his or her soul in the outside world. Some apprenticed themselves to craftsmen and learnt new trades. All worked for the good of the community and all activities were valued equally. Whatever their background, they would happily 'work' in the kitchen, garden, laundry or carpentry. They did not consider it 'work', but an offering from the heart to God. In all their activities they expressed creative love.

They were expert agriculturists and arboriculturists with a vast knowledge of crops, soil and climactic conditions, which enabled them to grow a variety of fruits and vegetables, with sophisticated drip irrigation systems to water the land.

Gardening for them was a study of the laws and forces of nature. It was a silent ritual, where they created the kingdom of heaven within themselves. The fruits and vegetables produced were a welcome by-product of their activities; but their real reward was in the knowledge, harmony and vitality they gained to enrich their lives.

All gave freely of their time and energy with no comparison and reckoning of another's contribution. Through harmony within the individual, the individual's spiritual evolution progressed steadily.

Membership in a community was possible only after a probationary period of one year and two further years of initiatory work. After the probationary year, the Candidate was permitted to wear the white gown, one of the distinguishing marks of an Essene. The next two years were spent studying and being tested. If successful, the candidate would surrender all personal possessions to the common store. The candidate then took the *Great Sevenfold Vow*, to never reveal the communions without permission, or to use the knowledge and power for material or selfish purposes. At this time he or she was accorded the honour of being admitted to the *Hadoth*, or secret meeting, where the deeper mysteries were revealed.

Communities were run under the concept of the 'One', or 'Teacher of Righteousness', the 'Three', the 'Council of Twelve', and the 'Council of the Many'. This was modelled on the 'Essene Tree of Life'. At the centre of the Tree of Life is a human being in meditation posture - the 'One' or 'Teacher of Righteousness'. The 'Three' were the three highest ranking priests and elected annually. They were represented by the three branches of the upper left portion of the Tree - Love, Wisdom and Power.

Each New Year, the 'Teacher of Righteousness' announced the names of those Essenes who would serve as 'The Council of Twelve'. Meetings began with beautiful songs, chants and recitations based on the Tree of Life Communions. The twelve moved in a circle around the Teacher of Righteousness, who is seated in the meditation posture at the centre. This is referred to in The Gospel of the Holy Twelve*, in regard to the 'Last Supper':

"And at evening the Master cometh into the house, and there are gathered with him the Twelve... And they were all clad in garments of white linen..."

"And when they had sung a hymn, Yeshua stood up in the midst of his apostles, and going round him who was their Centre, as in a solemn dance, they rejoiced..."

After the Tree of Life songs and rituals, the "business meeting" was held. In prayer, the group asked that the Centre Branch, God and the Centre Root, Mother Nature, be with them and guide all of their decisions at the meeting. In this way, all fourteen of the branches and roots were represented at the meetings: twelve by human beings, two by God and Mother Nature.

The Teacher of Righteousness was a lifelong position; the others served one year terms but could be reinstated at the New Year Naming Ceremony for another year.

Often they served many years, sometimes until death, as there was no limit to the number of consecutive one year terms they could serve.

*'The Gospel of the Holy Twelve' is an Aramaic text discovered in a Buddhist monastery in Tibet in 1870.

The Teacher of Righteousness would isolate his or herself for several days at the end of each year and do a fast. He or she would then invoke the presence of the Centre Branch, God, and the Centre Root, Mother Nature, and ask their guidance in the selection of the persons for the Council of Twelve for the upcoming year. Then, he or she went into a deep Communion with God and Mother Nature which culminated in the writing down of twelve names.

There is a symbolic connection between the 'Three', and the Spirit, mind and body. The Essenes believed their teachings provided a doorway into the ranks of angelic beings - the spiritual hierarchy protected the esoteric teachings from being watered down or disclosed to their enemies.

Sarah was the Teacher of Righteousness or 'One' at Lake Mareotis, and Mary, Anne and I were the Three. The Council of Twelve was chosen each New Year and the Council of the Many was made up of all good standing members of the community who wished to partake. This Council was involved with the smooth running of daily affairs at our community.

At Lake Mareotis we became known far and wide for our accomplishments in the field of healing. For this reason Lake Mareotis and the three other communities in Egypt were referred to as the *Therapeutae*.

Unlike other religious systems who scorned the physical body, we believed it was '*the Temple of the Living God*'. That the diseased elements of a sick body could be so touched by Divine Power, and cast out, through the creation of a spiritual atmosphere in which they could not remain.

Firstly, we believe that Divinity is expressed in the plant kingdom as an antidote for the illnesses of the animal kingdom - that for every illness of man there exists a palliative in a root, leaf or bark of a tree or plant. Furthermore, these healing properties had been placed there by the Divine Creator and were not merely the natural growth of the plant.

Over many years of experience we learned about and used many tools:

Nutrition - we were guided to use specific natural foods to prevent and heal certain diseases

Breathing exercises

Fasting - it gave the body an opportunity to regenerate and increased spiritual power

Massage - the healing power of human touch

Heliotherapy (sun therapy)

Hydrotherapy - the cleansing miracle of living pure water

Gardening - the healing power of being in touch with Mother Earth

The use of precious and semi-precious stones which affect the body's energy fields.

Crucially, we recognized the healing powers of the invisible worlds around us.

Through years of practice, we learned these invisible energies could be controlled by a trained and disciplined consciousness. In every instance, these energies were spiritually invoked, and few illnesses could withstand the application of the higher powers.

We had many visitors, some curious as to our way of living, but the majority sick in body, mind or both. In the words of Yeshua, *'first heal the body, and then the soul'.*

When Yeshua sent his apostles out he instructed them to be *'as wise as serpents, and harmless as doves'.* To be *'as wise as serpents'* refers to the attainment of wisdom or cosmic consciousness through the arousal of kundalini* up through the spine, to the spiritual and psychic centres of the head.

To be *'as harmless as doves'* refers to the striving of this objective with a purified consciousness. This 'serpent power' is incredibly powerful, and without pure or good intention, could be harmful.

The Essenes believed that through raising their consciousness and teaching the minority who understood and obeyed the Law, mankind would one day come to know the fourth peace of the Essenes, peace with humanity.

To achieve peace in the world was the ultimate collective aim of all Essene communities, including Lake Mareotis.

* Kundalini (coiled snake) in Hinduism, is a form of divine feminine energy (or Shakti) located at the base of the spine. When this energy is awakened, it may feel like electric current running up the spine, and is believed to lead to spiritual liberation.

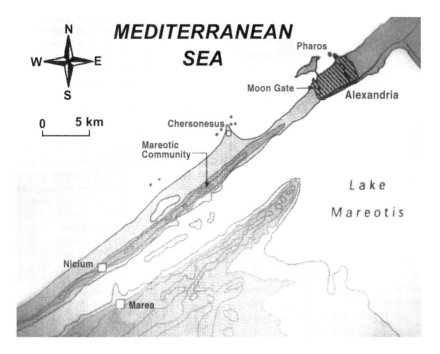

Figure 5: Map showing location of Lake Mareotis community, Alexandria, Egypt

Chapter VI

The Didache

September 87

My heart skipped a beat as I spotted the Pharos Lighthouse marking the entrance to Alexandria harbour. It was two years since I had left on my travels - I had had many experiences to savour and reflect on. My previous life in Alexandria seemed so distant now... Ironically it had saved me. My burdens had been transformed into blessings. I would not have got to spend time with four extraordinary men who helped to put me back on the path. And I would not have met Helena. So I had much to be thankful for.

I had written to Sarah to say I would be moving to Lake Mareotis with my new family. I had given her the date of our departure from Antioch, but the strength and direction of wind would determine the exact date of our arrival. I hired a donkey and cart at the quayside to take us and our few belongings to Lake Mareotis. I tingled with excitement when I caught sight of our community.

We were spotted from a watchtower which had been added to the corner of the main building. Sarah was alerted and she came running towards us, shouting,

"Jude and his family have arrived!"

She ran towards me and hugged me so hard I could hardly breathe. Sarah turned to me, staring into my face,

"Jude, how are you? We are so pleased to have you back!" I wondered if she meant physically, spiritually, or both but let it pass.

"Yes, Mother. I have much to share with you, but first you should meet my family!" Sarah immediately stepped back and turned to Helena to introduce herself. She directed her gaze to John Julius who was in her arms - he had been sleeping soundly but was stirring with the commotion. Mother gasped with delight when she set eyes upon him. He looked at her inquisitively with a steady gaze from his piercing blue eyes - the same as hers. He already had a soft downy head of blonde hair. Sarah gasped,

"What a handsome child! And the image of his beautiful mother!"

Helena smiled and handed our son to Sarah to hold. She cradled him in her arms and couldn't take her eyes off him. Father, Jean Claude and my sisters, Mary and Anne, appeared and after welcoming Helena, also cooed over John Julius.

I couldn't believe how much the community had grown! Land had been purchased to accommodate the increased number of cabins - Sarah said there were now 200 - 190 were occupied by community members and the rest for our frequent visitors - people passing through for days, weeks or sometimes months.

The main structure was now some 90 x 115 feet in size. It included meeting rooms, classrooms, a kitchen, and a room for copying and storing our writings. Around this building, connected by a system of channels, was a series of pools in which the Baptismal rites were performed.

The gardens had expanded, with an orchard of fruit trees and various vegetables growing in immaculate, orderly rows.

During the short rainy season, they channelled the rain water that poured down the ridge at Lake Mareotis into large cisterns for watering the rest of the year. Surplus food was taken to Alexandria to help feed the poor.

Mary excitedly showed us to our cabins, next to one another; six cabins clustered in a horseshoe shape for Sarah, Jean Claude, Mary, Anne, Helena and John Julius, and myself. A family compound. Helena and John Julius would share one cabin, and I would have my own.

Inside were three garments - a white robe which we covered with a linen shawl during the summer months, and a cloak of shaggy hide for the winter months. We had an additional white gown for festivals and ceremonies.

Mary, my eldest sister, offered to show Helena around the community. Mary was blessed with beauty, grace, wit and intelligence. More importantly she was also kind. She looked younger than her 29 years, as she wore her long silky brown hair in pig tails. She had not lost her child-like sense of fun; she would always be young at heart. She was friendly and belonged to everyone, and yet to no one.

She felt compassion for Helena leaving her family behind to join our community. I hoped they would become friends - I prayed every day that Helena would be happy here.

Anne had a lot of our mother Sarah's qualities; she was small, but stronger than her wiry build suggested. She was basically shy, quiet and uncomfortable in crowds. Anne had her grandmother's colouring; she had auburn hair and hazel brown eyes, which were so clear you could almost see your reflection in them.

Anne did not smile gratuitously, but when she did, her eyes became pools of love which could light up a whole room with their radiance. Her cool and capable disposition belied underlying anxiety.

She loved to work in the garden - it soothed her nerves. She was incapable of sitting still for long, and busied herself with sewing and mending. She disapproved of over sentimentality, bad time-keeping, sloppiness and laziness. She was self- critical, but could not accept criticism from others.

Anne was more reserved and studious than Mary - looking back she had probably been in Mary's shadow growing up, as Mary was more outgoing and her mere presence spread joy where ever she went.

Mary would have made a good mother but she had an unconscious fear that desire for one person would imprison her spirit in some way, and keep her from being true to her one great love - freedom. Freedom to serve humanity.

Anne had other gifts - she was blessed with a sharp intellect. While I was away Anne had been busy writing Codex VI - eight tractates making it the longest of all the codices.

It was customary in our community to baptize all new arrivals with the 'five seals' baptism ceremony. I was keen to show my writings to Sarah, particularly '*The Didache*', the guideline to running a Christian church or community I had written while I was in Antioch. Ours was a strict ascetic community and would not appeal to all - without being 'all things to all men', I had learnt from Polycarp that it was pragmatic to make some compromises in order to attract a wider following.

Unlike the churches I had visited in Rome and Antioch we had no bishops, presbyters or deacons.

Before our evening meal a president was elected, male or female, to discuss questions arising from the codices. We had much to discuss. Codices II, III and IV written by Mary Magdalene, Codices I and V written by Sarah, Codex VI written by my sister Anne, and Codex VIII written by my eldest sister Mary.

The president repeated the questions slowly so everyone could understand, explaining the texts with precise meaning, penetrating our souls. Sarah proposed I was the 'president' for the next few nights so I could read out *The Didache*; we could meditate on it, and the Council of Twelve could decide whether to adopt it.

The Didache

The Didache offered new communities and churches direction about how to accomplish Yeshua's command to his apostles to,

"Go forth from here. Make disciples of all people." *

*NT Matthew 28:19

The first line of The Didache reads,

"The teaching of the Lord to the Gentiles (or Nations) by the twelve apostles"

The Didache was based on my observations in Antioch of cultural tensions between the Jews and Gentiles, which had led to the disagreement between Peter and Paul. These issues had never been fully resolved and a 'code of conduct' would be helpful if the growth of the Christian church was to be harmonious.

I endeavoured to keep it as brief as possible and divided it into three sections; Forming New Disciples, Celebrating Christian Rituals and Governing the Community.

Forming New Disciples

'The Two Ways' is the ethical instruction that new initiates received in preparation for baptism before joining a community or church.

'The Two Ways' refer to the virtuous Way of Life and the Wicked Way of Death. This was necessary as many people came from a pagan background; adultery, sex with minors, eating sacrificed foods was considered 'normal' - of course they were all unacceptable behaviours to us.

Avoiding vice and choosing virtue, set the community of disciples apart from the society in which they lived. It was not intended to be in any way self-righteous; the 'Two Ways' was intended to engender a sense of sympathy for those who were on the path to spiritual death, and a sense of urgency about the mission to evangelize. To be aware of and compassionate towards the weakness of human nature; the disciple is urged to follow the way of life *'to the extent that one was able'*. There were no explicit restrictions on food, the new disciple was encouraged to judge for himself what food to eat, but to remain wary of food that had been sacrificed to idols as it may lead to slavery and worship of lifeless gods.

Celebrating Christian rituals

Baptism

We believe that baptism mirrors in the spiritual realm what takes place in the physical realm.

Baptism, the sacramental rite that admits someone to a Christian community, would be conferred in the name of the Father and of the Son, and of the Holy Spirit, with triple immersion in 'living water' (flowing water, a stream of river). It is important the water was 'living' or 'flowing', as the flowing water of a river, stream, or spring washed the individual clean of sin and filled him or her with new life in Christ. The person to be baptized would remove all their clothes before stepping into the baptismal water. If the water was insufficient for immersion, it would be poured three times on the head. The individual was immersed three times by the baptizer, and then given a clean robe to wear after emerging from the water. The baptized literally took off 'old humanity' and physically put on a 'new humanity'.

The Lord's Prayer

Christians should recite the Lord's Prayer at least three times a day, at times of their choosing.

Our Divine Father, blessed be Your Name!
May your Kingdom come,
That your will may be accomplished perfectly upon earth.
Gather us today at the Messiah's banquet.
Forgive our failings as we forgive those who fail us.
Do not let us be tested beyond our faith's endurance,
But protect us from all evil.
Power and glory are yours forever.
Amen.

Yeshua preached a renewed Covenant with God. He taught his disciples to expect, look forward to, and pray for a time when all would be fed by the wisdom and justice of God. Every line is a prayer that looks forward to the Lord's return in glory. The last three lines express a heartfelt desire to persevere in one's discipleship until the very end.

Sunday is the Sabbath day, the day of worship for Christian churches. Fasting should not be on Monday and Thursday *'with the hypocrites',* but on Wednesday and Sunday... *Hypocrites* referred to non-Christian Jews, such as the Pharisees.

There were two versions of the Eucharist or thanksgiving prayer, the central act of Christian worship, for use at the community's evening meal. Even in churches this was an actual meal, as was the Lord's Supper. I was influenced by Pope Clement of Rome, who wanted to offer baptized Christians a meal, so they would not have to beg in the street, as his mother had done.

I had observed in my travels that all communities and churches experienced disagreements, misunderstandings and conflict. For Christianity to survive unity was to be prized above all else, and our shared expectation of our Lord's return was a uniting force emphasised in the thanksgiving prayer recited at the end of the meal.

A blessing of God for sustaining the universe, who gives the gifts of food, earth and covenant, and a prayer for the restoration of Jerusalem. I had learnt this prayer from Bishop Ignatius of Antioch.

Governing a Community

Itinerant, or travelling, apostles and prophets were of great importance, some of whom were invited to serve as 'chief priests' and conduct the Eucharist. I offered guidelines on how to differentiate a genuine prophet that deserves support from a false prophet - principally by his character and actions.

One should welcome every itinerant prophet as one would welcome the Lord. Let him stay one day, but no more than two days.

If he remains a third day he is a false prophet, seeking to exploit the community's generosity. If he wishes to reside among you, and is skilled at a craft, allow him to do so.

When the prophet leaves, he should be given enough food for the rest of the day; if he asks for money he is a false prophet. A prophet who teaches the truth but does not put it into practice is a false prophet. A prophet asking for food for the poor would not eat it himself, unless he was a false prophet.

One should not judge the statements of a prophet who has been proved authentic when he enters an ecstatic state, unless he tries to teach others to imitate him. He is to be judged only by God, as in the time of the ancient prophets. The leader of the congregation should encourage the prophets to give thanks, that is, pray, for an unspecified length of time.

Church leadership consisted of bishops and deacons, gradually superseding the itinerant ministry. Leaders and assistants should be elected who are worthy before the Lord; humble, truthful and reliable as they serve as your prophets and teachers. They should be respected and held in high esteem. But to also remember that not all those drawn to ministry embrace these virtues.

Christians were invited to gather on Sunday to break bread, but in order that their offering was pure, they should confess their sins first, as well as reconcile any grievances with others.

To pray, give alms and perform good works according to the example seen in the Good News of Our Lord.

I end *The Didache* with a warning; in the final days there will be many false prophets, sheep will be transformed into wolves, and love transformed into hate. Many will falter and perish, but those who stand firm in their faith will be saved by our Lord.

I said Helena and I would like to prepare for baptism by fasting for two days prior to the ceremony. It would be preferable for Sarah, as the baptizer, and members of the community, to also fast. It was a cleansing, a form of offering to our Father by the whole community.

After our two day fast, we rose at dawn to pray before silently proceeding to the lake shore, where we waited for all our members to assemble. We slipped off our gowns and entered the water to chest height, with Helena holding John Julius. Sarah came towards us and baptized me first, immersing me three times, blessing me with the Father, the Son and the Holy Spirit. Tears streamed down my face as I watched my wife and young son being baptized. Helena handed John Julius to Sarah and he looked a little puzzled as Sarah briefly immersed him, but he did not cry. Children are from heaven after all, so he probably understood on a soul level. I looked at Sarah and saw two swollen tears meandering down her face - I had never seen my mother cry but these were tears of joy. It was a very emotional moment for all of us - John Julius was the only one with dry eyes.

We emerged from the shallows and donned our ceremonial robes to be greeted by the whole community - they clapped and cheered for us and we felt elated. It was a new beginning for us, and I had great hopes for the future.

Helena seemed to settle in well. The way of life at our community was a far cry from the privileged background she had come from, but for most of us the spiritual blessings far outweighed any physical discomfort. Even so, two years ago I had been riddled with doubt as to whether the spiritual life was for me.

Helena had the patience of a saint and enough self-control to hold back a team of horses. But it was a big ask - she had been dropped in the deep end and nobody had taught her how to swim.

Chapter VII

Alexandria and Antioch

My father, Jean Claude, was still running his cabinet making business in Alexandria. He visited often and Sarah predicted our arrival would speed up his retirement plans. It was just a question of time.

I took Helena to visit my family home in Alexandria and the workshop where I had spent many hours learning my father's trade - the smell of the sawdust was like a child's comfort blanket to me. Running home from school to be where my heart was - in the workshop with father, initially being much more of a hindrance than a help, no doubt. Father was so patient - if I was half as good a father to John Julius as Father had been to me, I would be a happy man.

Jean Claude was very sweet to Helena and spent hours talking to her, asking about Antioch and her upbringing. He understood what it was like to be uprooted from one's own family and culture and be transported hundreds of miles away.

Sarah and Jean Claude were concerned about the strain on a young married couple of having no intimacy, as we had separate cabins at the community. They had experienced the same, but were older and had been married some time by then. It was Jean Claude's idea that we should spend one night a week at our home in Alexandria with him - it would be our date night! John Julius would sleep with Jean Claude and I would share a bed and a whole night with my beautiful wife. I would wake up before her in the morning and just gaze at her angelic face as dawn came and the sun blazed through our bedroom window.

But it was always a wrench for her to return to Lake Mareotis. She didn't say anything, but she was always quiet on our way back to the community. I was torn. I had other responsibilities and work to do at the community.

Jean Claude supervised and helped with the maintenance of the community buildings. The climate took its toll on our wooden cabins, so there was much to be done and he needed my assistance. We enjoyed working together, serving our community in a real and practical way. We were especially busy before the winter approached, as we wanted to ensure the buildings were water tight as well as wind proof.

There were external threats to our community too. Bandits were an occasional problem - they knew we had no valuables and so would only come if they were hungry, on their way to richer pickings in Alexandria. The lookout tower and two dogs served to alert us of any unwelcome nocturnal visitors - we were unarmed of course, so the dogs were our guards.

Greek Jewish relations in Alexandria were dictated by the line taken by the Roman Governor of Egypt - if he turned a 'blind eye' to anti-Jewish behaviour, the Greeks felt they had been given tacit permission to abuse the Jewish community and violence would escalate. The majority of people were living under cramped, insanitary conditions and took their frustrations out on whoever crossed their path. This made stonings all too common, particularly in the agora. The current Governor was more sympathetic to the Greeks than the Jews. Trips to the market became more perilous, our women never travelled alone and never after dusk. We kept our heads down, travelled in small groups, and avoided the agora if possible.

But there were problems within the community as well. These were a bigger threat and harder to deal with, although Sarah was quick to settle any disagreements before they festered and grew into cankers.

We were an egalitarian spiritual community, but disagreements, misunderstandings and conflicts arose from time to time. It was not an easy option being on the path - a life-long commitment with little physical comfort. Jealousy and rivalry would rear their ugly heads on a regular basis. Judgement of others was divisive and encouraged gossip. We had no possessions, so envy of friendships, power struggles, another person's spiritual gifts, ability to deliver the evening treatise, speaking in tongues and prophesising, could ruffle feathers.

Visiting prophets could upset the equilibrium with their 'gifts' - impressing our newer members and forming splinter groups. They would visit almost daily, some were authentic, some were not, and would ask for money.

Sarah was amazing at resolving these issues, in her calm, non-judgemental, unflappable way. It was part of the human condition to be subject to the whole spectrum of emotions. Our training was to focus on the positive emotions. Mother emphasised tolerance, forgiveness, self-control and handing our problems over to God. Unity was valued above all, and was essential to ensure our survival. We all shared the same expectation of our Lord's return in glory.

She reminded us to pray and perform good works according to the Good News of our Lord. In a nutshell, to think good, be good and do good.

To settle all quarrels and disagreements before evening prayers, so one did not kneel to pray with a burden on one's conscience.

To let no one lead us to stray from this path of discipleship. If we were able to do all these things in communion with the Lord, we would be perfect. This was our goal. But others had only walked the path for a short time, and would inevitably stumble or stray. So we prayed for them, as they deserve to be prayed for, and aimed to love them more than we loved ourselves.

Living in a mixed community, sexual attraction and physical relations were another temptation and distraction from our path. Sensuality and carnal pleasures took us away from our inner work and were not permitted. Lustful thoughts and lewd conversations could lead to sexual promiscuity. Those who secretly partook in relations were asked to leave - they could return if they felt able to be chaste and ready to walk our path again. Some returned, others did not, a celibate life was not for everyone.

As the 'Three', my sisters and I supported Sarah in running the community, but I was grateful not to be the leader. This day would arrive in due course, but hopefully not for some time.

January 88

After Helena, John Julius and I came to live at Lake Mareotis, Jean Claude could not bear to miss out on being with his grandson, and decided to retire so he could come to live with us at the community. He sold half of his business to Marcus, one of his long-standing employees, who I had known since I was a boy and worked with during my apprenticeship. Marcus said there would always be an opening for me if I ever wished to return to 'normal' life - unlikely, but it was a kind offer which I appreciated.

Jean Claude took a few months to arrange matters and came to live at the community in the new year of 88. John Julius had settled in very quickly. He had everything of course. He was showered with love not only by his parents, aunts and grandparents, but the entire community.

Sarah loved to watch him - she said he was having the same upbringing she had had in her first nine years, albeit without her beloved Philo who tutored her. She said our Lord would send someone when the time was right - I had to remind her that John Julius was only six months old and would not need a tutor for a few years yet...

Sadly, with the sale of Jean Claude's business, we bade farewell to our family home. Our weekly visits to Alexandria came to an end - Helena missed these terribly. She could not bear weakness of any kind, in herself or others. She said nothing, but I could see it in her eyes - there was loneliness and isolation gazing back at me, and I was unable to console her. As I had promised before we left Antioch, I said I would take her home to see her family in late spring, when the winds settled down, and it was a little warmer. I knew this was not a solution, as it would only be for a few weeks, but at least it would give her something to look forward to.

Mary and Anne tried to engage her in helping with the running of the community; she would go through the motions, but you could see her heart was not in it. Helena enjoyed going for walks barefoot along the lake shore with Mary and John Julius; Mary's enthusiasm and delight in the baby was infectious - that was the happiest I saw her really.

If I tried to talk to Helena about my concerns, she just refused to discuss the matter. She was born under Taurus the bull - she was as stubborn as a human could be without actually turning into stone. She was steady, solid and did not wish to be disturbed. She would not be pushed. Her impassivity to emotional stress was remarkable.

She had not complained once since we had arrived at Lake Mareotis. Her loyalty and devotion to her family was of supreme importance to her. That was now me, John Julius and life at Lake Mareotis.

Helena did not remind me, but it was time for me to fulfil my promise of taking her home to her family in Antioch that summer.

In the meantime, I threw myself into my writing - it was an escape and coping strategy to begin with, taking me away from my day to day problems. My first transmission at Lake Mareotis was *The Second Discourse of Great Seth*, the second tractate of codex VII.

June 88

Helena, John Julius and I left Alexandria harbour on a fine, sunny morning, to sail back to Seleucia. Helena's spirits lifted as the Egyptian coastline disappeared out of sight and we sailed north towards her homeland. It was two years since I had first arrived in Seleucia after leaving John in Patmos - so much had happened... I had a wife and one year old son now.

Ruth and Aaron were waiting on the dock and waved excitedly as we came alongside the quay in the inner harbour. With John Julius in her arms, Helena ran down the gangway and hugged them both for a long time. The strain of living at Lake Mareotis for the last nine months, seemed to vanish from her face almost immediately. Her mother, Ruth looked at her and said,

"Helena, you have lost weight! We will have to put that right!"

"Oh mother, I am absolutely fine, I am still breastfeeding and John Julius is a hungry child!" she replied. This did nothing to allay Ruth's fears,

"Well, you need a balanced diet - plenty of fish, meat and fresh vegetables!" This was an unveiled reference to our meat free diet at Lake Mareotis.

We made our way to their home in Antioch and Helena showed John Julius around her family home - rather different to our cabins at the community. I had not actually stayed at her family home, as we had moved into our rented house after our wedding. I had not realized the luxury she was accustomed to. Her bathroom resembled Cleopatra's private quarters, the shelves stocked with oils and lotions.

Helena was a different woman. She got her vitality back, chatted over meals and wanted to go on lots of walks with me and John Julius.

Ruth had hired a nursemaid for the duration of our stay, so we could have time together on our own. We would be able to indulge her love of art and music. She had missed the grand buildings of Antioch and loved strolling around the city centre. Helena was blessed with a beautiful singing voice - Ruth had bought us tickets for a concert at Daphne Park, where I had proposed to her.

Ignatius was delighted to see us of course; he made a big fuss over John Julius, as everyone did. He invited me round on my own, supposedly to update me on the developments in the church community. His agenda was not as I had expected.

"Ah, I see all is not well with your family, Jude" he said soberly. I could never hide anything from Ignatius. I went quiet - I did not know what to say, but did not need to say anything. I could be completely honest with Ignatius and knew it would remain between these four walls.

"She has never really settled in... I do not know what to do anymore. She is so different here, her old self. I feel guilty about taking her away from here - she is not happy." I lowered my head and Ignatius paused for a few moments.

"Well you don't have many options. She could return home, but you could not bear to be parted from John Julius, and I am sure your parents would not accept that. I have a friend with a house in Alexandria - I could ask him if you might stay there from time to time?"

"That is very kind, Ignatius. But she doesn't have any friends there and it is not safe for her to wander around the city. The governor is not very supportive to the Jewish community presently." Ignatius continued,

"Yes, I see. Well she clearly loves you. Are you writing again?" I nodded.

"Get her involved in your work, discuss it with her and ask her to make copies for you. She is more than just a mother you know - your grandmother will be shaking her head!"

"But she is not an intellectual, Ignatius, she is much more of a practical person", I argued.

"Maybe not, but she is no fool either. From the time I spent with her I observed her ideas were sensible, and could sparkle with deep clarity and depth. She always grasped the fundamentals of any subject." I nodded in agreement, marvelling at Ignatius' insight into my dear wife.

I said I would discuss it with her. Ignatius was right, of course. I had seen her mainly as a mother, her role as a wife was somewhat different at the community. And yes, Mary Magdalene would be shaking a disapproving finger at me!

"What did you want to tell me about the local churches Ignatius?"

I enquired. "Oh that was just a ruse to get you on my own!" he retorted, laughing.

I smiled to myself. He was such a wise man. Or I was a fool. He wasn't even married and yet clearly he had more idea about women than I did. I couldn't help but laugh at myself!

"What are you laughing about? Are you going to share your little joke?", he burst out, slapping me on the back. He knew of course - he could see the relief on my face.

I returned to Helena's home with a spring in my step. I shared with her my conversation with Ignatius and she greeted the idea with enthusiasm - we would also get to spend more time together. I felt my prayers had at least been listened to.

Helena was very much a physical creature, but needed sensual satisfaction from everything around her. The scent of freshly washed sheets saturated with the sweet smell of sunshine, or the delicious aroma of freshly baked bread made her happy beyond belief!

John Julius was taken care of, so that evening we took an oil scented bath together, then lay on her bed massaging each other with ylang ylang oil.

I was patient, waiting until she begged me to enter her. We made love several times that night, at first with a sense of urgency, and then slowly with tenderness, joy and sheer delight in one another. We had not experienced this since the early days of our marriage.

I held her in my arms until we drifted into delicious sleep. In the morning, I awoke before her and gazed at her face for a long time, drinking in her beauty. My stomach wheeled with delight and I fell in love with her all over again. She was precious, and I had to take better care of her.

On our last evening in Antioch, Aaron took me to one side,

"Jude, will you promise to write to me if Helena continues to be unhappy at your community? She will never complain - she has inherited my sense of stoicism and fear of weakness which will not allow her to. She is not as strong as you think, and we are worried about her." I turned to him,

"Sir, we have all been worried about her. I will do what you ask. Please be sure that I love her deeply and will take good care of your daughter and grandson. We will return every summer so they can spend time with you and Ruth."

Sadly, I would not keep my promise, and my last words to Aaron would haunt me for a long time.

Chapter VIII

Hope for the Future

July 88

As long as I lived, the welcome sight of Pharos Lighthouse towering above us would never fail to impress me, and signalled our safe return to Alexandria.

Jean Claude was there at the quay to greet us, with Pico the donkey standing patiently to attention, nonchalantly munching on hay. Jean Claude embraced us both, but his eyes were on John Julius, who had his arms stretched out in anticipation. Jean Claude threw him into the air several times, as John Julius squealed with delight. Jean Claude grinned from ear to ear.

I saw him glance sideways at Helena to see if there was a change in her after our trip. Everyone was concerned about her. She looked better - she had put on some weight, but more importantly, there was a light behind her eyes again. Helena held John Julius on her lap, as I excitedly pointed out the local sights, just as Sarah had done when we were growing up.

I realised that you only really appreciate your parents when you become a parent yourself, the many sacrifices they make which you are completely unaware of. The whole world revolves around you when you are young, until you have a child, when your child becomes the focus. That's when I started to really grow up... I am still learning about women, and am beginning to realize that may well be a life-long process!

Sarah and the girls were there to greet us as Pico trotted proudly through the community entrance - the guard dogs had alerted them of our imminent arrival.

It was mid-afternoon and so we had time to go for a walk before evening prayers. Sarah said she would like to accompany us, as she had something to discuss with us.

She said she had been concerned from the outset about the strain of a celibate relationship on a newly married couple, and had some suggestions she would like to share. She had learnt this in the mystery schools. She had not disclosed this earlier as firstly, she had been sworn to secrecy, and secondly, did not want to be seen to be giving her son and daughter-in-law preferential treatment. Well, nothing could have prepared me for what she was about to say.

Sarah went onto say that it was possible to have sexual relations on an energetic level that did not involve any physical contact. Her and father had practised it for years - it had kept their marriage alive and she could heartily recommend it. I looked down at my sandals - no one wants to talk about sex with one's parents... Helena looked intrigued.

Mother explained that it was known as the Tantra in the esoteric traditions of Hinduism and Buddhism. The energy was *kundalini*, a form of divine feminine energy, located at the base of the spine.

In Ancient Egypt, it was known as the Sex Magic of Isis, or the Alchemy of Horus, depending on whether it was practised with a partner or solo.

Sexual energy could be directed in specific ways through breathing and visualization techniques to reach a higher level of being, and a sustained feeling of ecstasy, which could give us a glimpse of what it felt like to be connected to the Divine. When this energy is awakened, it feels like electric current running up the spine, and can lead to spiritual liberation. Connection to the Divine also offers protection against the dark energies which lead us away from the path.

It was believed in ancient Egypt that the orgasm was the key to eternal life. Most people are unaware of what happens to their sexual energy after they have an orgasm. Usually the energy moves up the spine and out of the top of the head.

Less often, the sexual energy is released down the spine into the hidden centre below the feet. In both cases, the sexual energy, the concentrated life-force energy, is lost.

So the ancients believed that orgasm brought one a little closer to death because a person loses his or her life-force energy in the orgasm. For this reason, in tantric practice the male was asked not to ejaculate. They also believed that if this energy was controlled by consciousness and breath control, the life force was not lost - it could re-enter the spine and continue to resonate and vibrate like a tuning fork. In fact it seemed to increase the amount of life-force energy. So, orgasm became a source of infinite life energy that not only connected one to one's own Divine self, but could lead to eternal life.

Sarah emphasised the importance of practice, but even if we tried it for just one week, we would notice a difference in the vitality and strength of our mental, emotional and physical bodies. It would increase our etheric or light bodies as well, with further practice we could practice relations with our light bodies which would not require us to even be in the same room!

At this point you could have blown me over with a feather. Sarah concluded,

"I think that is more than enough information for one afternoon. If you wish to explore this, tomorrow I will give you specific instructions on the breath control and direction of consciousness - the timing is key. Well we don't want to be late for evening prayers - we should get back!" She turned on her heels and headed back to her cabin. I watched her for some time with incredulity; there was much more to this woman than I could ever have imagined.

And so our daily lessons began. Sarah did not know how long it would take - it was different for everyone. We were to practice daily. Even from the beginning, I could feel the difference between this experience and physical sex, it was a whole new world. Sarah suggested I went to Jean Claude with any 'technical' questions and Helena came to her - for obvious reasons.

What fun we had!

After morning prayers I would return to my cabin to resume my writing. My next transmission was *The Revelation of Peter*, tractate three of codex VII. Helena, Mary and Anne made copies for me. On our afternoon 'walks' Helena would have many questions - suddenly we had so much to talk about! And we never skipped our homework.

After a few weeks of daily instruction Sarah said we were on our own from then on, and said it was down to intention, focus and practice. It had opened up a whole new world of experience for us both, we both felt so *vital* and alive!

We had to be creative and hide from John Julius sometimes, which made us feel like dating teenagers, and only added to the excitement. We never felt guilty as there was always someone to play with him. Now toddling around aged 14 months, he was adventurous and mischievous. He had no fear. He would look up at you with his blond curls framing his round face and imploring blue eyes - few could resist his requests! Sarah didn't have the energy to run after him, but was always ready to read John Julius a story when he was tired.

And so life continued at Lake Mareotis. We were all very busy - running a community takes a lot of work and organization, but when we were in harmony, it seemed effortless. 'Problems' arose from time to time, but quickly became 'no problem'.

Lessons were learned each and every day, either from our fellow members or visiting prophets or travellers. At morning prayers, Sarah would remind us of the virtues we should all be striving for, gratitude, honesty and humility.

Written on the community hall wall was the quote from Cicero, the Roman philosopher who lived from 106-43 BC,

Gratitude is not only the greatest of virtues, but the parent of all others."

It certainly leads to humility, to never consider you are better than your fellow man. Honesty is paramount; above all being honest with oneself, in order to be honest with one's fellow man. If one is not truthful, then it is akin to dancing on quicksand - there is no foundation and no direction.

To not fake any spiritual gifts, pretending to talk in tongues for example, in order to impress someone.

To not judge our fellow man, for that is not our jurisdiction. That is for God. It is so easy to see faults in others, but often they are mirroring our own flaws, and have been sent to bring them to our awareness, to shine a light in a dark corner so more cleaning can be done. So instead of being offended or hurt by someone, we should be grateful to them, as it is an insight or lesson for us. To see everything as a blessing, sometimes in disguise.

This road is long and difficult; with prayer and meditation we are able to look into the very core of our being. We meet wounds that do not want to be reopened and can be very painful. They were buried for a reason. But this part is very fertile and where real transformation and growth can take place. The rewards justify the effort. It is the only worthwhile work. The inner work is not visible, but manifests in the outer world. We can make this world a better place.

I then wrote *The Teachings of Silvanus* and *The Three Steles of Seth* to complete Codex VII. Each tractate took around three months to write - the first draft took little time, but then I would discuss it with Helena before delivering excerpts in the evening discourse - I valued my fellow members' opinions. We were a united community after all.

I was not the only one writing; in 86 whilst I had been in Antioch, Mary had written *Zostrianos*, the first tractate of Codex VIII. This is a mighty work, a lengthy account of a vision received by a man named *Zostrianos*, of the emanations that are produced by God in esoteric cosmological language. Various baptisms mark the stripping away of worldly concerns and a resultant vision of transcendent reality and a 'knowledge of the All'.

Mary recognized that this would not be read by the masses, and in 88 wrote *The Sentences of Sextus*, the first tractate of Codex XII. This is a collection of 610 sayings. Simple, and to the point. After all, spiritual teachings can seem complicated and result in further complicating an already complicated world. Here are some of my favourites:-

- Everything God possesses, the wise man has also.

- Let the moment come before your words.

- While it is a skill to speak, it is also a skill to be silent.

- Wisdom guides the soul to God.

- The fear of death grieves man because of the ignorance of the soul.

- Don't let an ungrateful person make you stop doing good.

- You cannot acquire understanding unless you first know you do not have it.

- Say in your heart that the body is the garment of the soul. Keep it pure, since it is innocent.

- Let your deeds of love for God come before all your words about God.

- Death cannot destroy.

I had no plans to visit foreign lands any more - my work was here. There were other disciples who travelled great distances in the name of the Lord.

We were still visited frequently by itinerant prophets. All were welcomed, but we learned to be cautious. Some of their ideas were quite outlandish. It was generally not a problem for our community being under Sarah's steadfast leadership, but I was concerned about the more fledgling and vulnerable communities.

It prompted me to write *Letter of Jude** to be circulated and read in all churches. I opened the letter with the line,

"Jude, a servant of Yeshua and brother of James" - I knew James would be thought to be James the Just, a prominent leader in the Church and brother of Yeshua. This in turn would make the author Jude also a brother of Yeshua and his testimony significant. Well, they were brothers of Yeshua in the way that we are all brothers and sisters, but not by blood.

The *Letter of Jude* is brief, a single chapter with 25 verses. I warned believers of the doctrine of certain errant teachers to whom they have been or may be exposed to. I urged readers to defend Yeshua's doctrine, to remember the words of the apostles, the most reliable witnesses to the word of our Lord, and to keep themselves in God's love.

I was drawn back to Mary Magdalene's *Gospel of John* and wrote *The Prologue to The Gospel of John.*

Prologue to the Gospel of John

In the beginning was the Word, and the Word was with God, and the Word was God. He was in the beginning with God.

All things came into being through Him, and apart from Him nothing came into being that has come into being.

In Him was life, and the life was the Light of men.

The Light shines in the darkness, and the darkness did not comprehend it.

*Letter of Jude is the penultimate book of the New Testament.

There came a man sent from God, whose name was John.

He came as a witness, to testify about the Light, so that all might believe through him.

He was not the Light, but he came to testify about the Light.

There was the true Light which, coming into the world, enlightens every man.

He was in the world, and the world was made through Him, and the world did not know Him.

He came to His own, and those who were not His own did not receive Him.

But as many as received Him, to them He gave the right to become children of God, even to those who believe in His name, who were born, not of blood nor of the will of the flesh nor of the will of man, but of God.

And the Word became flesh, and dwelt among us, and we saw His glory, glory as the only begotten from the Father, full of grace and truth.

John testified about Him and cried out, saying, "This was He of whom I said, 'He who comes after me has a higher rank than I, for He existed before me.'"

For of His fullness we have all received, and grace upon grace.

For the Law was given through Moses; grace and truth were realized through Yeshua.

No one has seen God at any time; the only begotten God who is in the bosom of the Father, He has explained Him.

The *Prologue to the Gospel of John* is a mystical reflection on the Divinity and incarnation of Yeshua, the Word made Flesh. The

Prologue begins and ends in eternity, with the Word entering time and history through Yeshua. Yeshua is the logos, the Word or reason, God's unifying concept for all creation.

Themes such as light, life, darkness, witness, faith, glory and truth are developed throughout the *Gospel of John*, transmitted by my grandmother, Mary Magdalene, over thirty years earlier.

The principle of the Incarnation would become the guiding theme for the *Gospel of John*, so that we distinguish Yeshua of Nazareth from 'the Son who comes from the Father,' a mystery that reveals itself in Yeshua as the Son of God.

I showed the *Prologue to the Gospel of John* to Sarah before I shared it with the community - I was a little apprehensive. Helena had loved it, asking me to read it to her again and again. But then she was my wife and my most loyal supporter. I was not prepared for Sarah's reaction. She was not prone to showing a lot of emotion, her mother Mary Magdalene had made many sacrifices in her lifetime, and did not show or expect any praise or sympathy.

She stood erect as she read it to herself. Then she was silent for what felt like an age. As she turned to look at me, I saw she had uncharacteristic tears silently rolling down her face. She slowly took hold of my hands and said almost inaudibly,

"Jude, your words have taken my breath away. This is beautiful, truly poetic and profound in nature. I am sure this will survive throughout the ages and be a guiding light for those who go on to read Mary Magdalene's *Gospel of John*".

"Thank you Mother, but we both know, these words are coming *through* me, not *from* me!". It was a glib reply, but inside I was glowing. I would savour this moment for years to come, in moments when the self-doubt would creep in. She then said,

"Jude, I have been thinking for some time about who should

take over the community when I leave here... I would need to discuss this with Mary and Anne, as I have always considered you equals, but my heart tells me you should be my successor". I was shaken out of my reverie, somehow stuttering a response,

"That would be an honour, Mother". But inside I felt queasy, a deep seated fear of living up to my mother and grandmother as leader of the community.

Mother would leave big shoes to fill.

Chapter IX

Helena and Eve

June 90

There was no time at the community. We were outside time... When I was writing I was immersed in another world, another dimension which made my heart and whole being sing.

John Julius was the only yardstick of time. He had turned 3 in June 90 - where had those years gone? I thought I had better spend more time with him before he turned 21 and wanted to make his own way in the world. He was expected to marry of course, given his bloodline. As great grandson, he was the only male heir to Yeshua and Mary Magdalene.

On his third birthday, my sister Mary asked Helena and I if she could be his tutor. She was always playing with him, so he loved her to pieces. Thanks to Sarah, we had all had a first class education here in Alexandria, so she was more than capable of teaching a three year old. Mary said she would go to the Serapeum and borrow books.

Helena and I did not hesitate for a second, but would have to defer to Sarah as leader of the community, but more importantly his grandmother. Sarah had reservations. Her tutor had been the renowned Philo of Alexandria, a highly educated Jewish philosopher who visited the community in its infancy, and became fascinated by Mary Magdalene's teachings. Philo had asked Mary Magdalene to baptize him, and sometime later, she in turn had asked him to be Sarah's tutor. Philo was like a father to Sarah, and she talked often of him, although she saw little of him after the age of nine when she left Alexandria for Gaul.

So the bar was set pretty high.

We argued that John Julius was only three, he wasn't training to be a physician, yet! Sarah said she was going to offer it up to our Lord, and suggested we all did the same. Mary for one was confident of how her prayers would be answered.

And so it was agreed that Mary would tutor John Julius on a trial basis, and if it was successful, could continue until his seventh year, when he would be old enough to attend the Serapeum school in Alexandria. This was when I started, although we were living in Alexandria at the time and it was only a short walk from our home. I decided it was premature to worry about these practical details for now.

Before Mary Magdalene and her inner circle had fled from the community in 43, she had placed Sarah's few belongings and school books in a chest. Sarah retrieved it from our storage room and had a wonderful time going through them, reminiscing about her days with Philo, making suggestions to Mary and telling her the games Philo played with her.

At 32, Mary was a lot younger than Philo had been, and had boundless energy - she pranced around the place, exuding life and vitality with a big smile on her beautiful face.

Helena and I took it in turns to read bed time stories to John Julius. That was my favourite time with him. To have a sleepy, warm child nestled in beside you, is truly one of life's great pleasures. First, John Julius would tell us about his day, with his bright blue eyes ablaze with his latest discovery or realization. It is such a privilege to see the world through a child's eyes; to witness the trust, innocence and sense of wonder. In the words of Yeshua,

"Except ye become as little children, ye shall not enter into the kingdom of heaven".

We started to introduce him to the great sights of Alexandria. The zoo was his favourite, just as it had been mine. As Sarah had done with us, we shielded him from the less savoury sights in Alexandria - it could be a dangerous place and we were cautious. On top of that we were Christians, so there were always those prepared to throw a stone at us. We kept our heads down and covered; we felt protected, but made every attempt to avoid any sort of trouble.

It was a magical time, we were happy beyond measure. But nothing lasts for ever.

February 91

The winters were not harsh in Alexandria. Temperatures rarely fell below 10'C in the winter months of December through February. December was the wettest and January the coldest. Of course, we had no form of heating in our cabins. For most of us this was not a problem; prayer and meditation has a beneficial effect on the whole body, the organs work more efficiently, the blood flows well, and so we built up an 'inner sacred fire' - we just didn't seem to feel the cold or damp.

Before Philo joined our community, he had referred to our community as the *Therapeutae*, as we performed healing of the mind, body and soul better than he had witnessed in any spa in Alexandria. Anywhere he had travelled, actually.

When necessary, we used herbs for common ailments, coughs, colds and mild infections. Mary Magdalene had taught Sarah about herbs and concoctions when she was still a young girl - Sarah loved to help her collect them either from the countryside or from the market.

We were no stranger to, and had no fear of death. Many of our older members died peacefully at our community, having spent many years there. For us there was no death, just 'passing on' to the next realm. The elderly and infirm were given constant and devoted care until their souls left their bodies. Without fear and pain, 'death' was as natural as going to sleep and awakening in another realm.

However, our minds and conditioning tell us there should be a natural order of things; old people die before young people right? This is one of the many tricks the mind plays on us; the soul never gets wrinkles, only the body, and sometimes the soul chooses to leave earlier than expected.

It happened so quickly. Helena was ill for less than a week, starting one Sunday in early February, with a chill and aching limbs, which rapidly developed into pneumonia. The herbs could do nothing to touch her raging fever. She suffered delirious night sweats, vomiting - she could not eat or keep any fluids down. One of the family was with her at all times, mopping her brow or holding her hand.

Mary took John Julius to sleep with her in her cabin - it was distressing and confusing for him to see his mother delirious, particularly at night. I felt so powerless; Sarah said all we could do was pray and accept God's will. She must have known that Helena would not recover, but did not say. I would not have listened anyway.

Helena knew as well. Near the end she regained consciousness and beckoned for me to come closer as her voice was weak,

"Thank you Jude... you were the love of my life... I will miss you and John Julius unbelievably... I know John Julius will be well looked after, it is you I am worried about! You are only 27 and must find happiness again... I beg of you!"

I put my finger on her lips to silence her, I could not bear to hear her speak this way,

"Shush, my dearest, all will be well... we need to trust in God".

But she was right... She left her body on Friday 9th February 91. She was just 25 years old. Before dawn, we carried her out of her cabin on a bier and buried her under a palm tree near the perimeter fence where she would have both shade and peace. Jean Claude made a wooden cross with the following inscription;

Helena du Bois aged 25, loving wife to Jude and mother to John Julius. 18.5.65 - 9.2.91.

That evening I wrote to Ruth and Aaron - the most difficult letter I have ever written. So much for my promise to her father Aaron - I feared they would not wish to see me again, and who could blame them?

I felt guilty. Her spirit had been crushed by living at Lake Mareotis. She had borne a brave face, but her soul had found a way of escape. I was truly heartbroken - I had lost my first true love. Heartache is a real physical pain. I wanted to rip my heart out of my chest so I couldn't feel the pain anymore... My grief raged inside like a wild animal. I was angry with God, so angry - what was the point of all this? I went for lots of walks and sobbed like a child in my cabin. I was inconsolable. Sarah spared me from advice and platitudes. She did not remind me that her mother Mary Magdalene had watched her beloved Yeshua die on the cross, whilst she was pregnant with her. That was the reason we were here. I felt like I was the only one suffering.

I am not sure when the grief merged into self-pity, but I can tell you that it was John Julius who saved me. Rescued me from my torment, and reminded me why I had a reason to live. I was neglecting my son. He was four months short of his fourth birthday and did not understand death, but he knew Helena was not coming back, and also missed her terribly. Now it must seem like he had lost his father too...

John Julius taught me to laugh again. In fact he brought me back to life. At just three years old, he took me by the hand and led me out of this dark place I had allowed myself to spiral into.

Before bedtime we would stare into the clear night sky, and tell Helena all about our day. John Julius talked in such a matter of fact way, with love and no fear of upsetting me. As if she was still alive, which she was, albeit in another dimension. John Julius had grasped the concept with little difficulty, I was desperately trying to catch up. This was a big lesson for me. Death and separation are an illusion; Helena had moved onto another plane but was with us all the time, just not in her physical body.

I did not write for some time after Helena died. After all the writing I had done, I was clearly unable to 'walk the talk' and felt ashamed. It gave me more compassion for those who fall off the path - life it is not easy, but then why do we expect it to be?

I spent more time with John Julius and helped Father with the buildings maintenance. Spring was in the air and it felt good to be outside. Father had built a make shift workshop which became my refuge where I retreated when I felt overwhelmed with grief. The smell of sawn wood never failed to soothe me. It felt good to be working with wood again, doing something physical. It was a form of therapy. Grief is a natural process and takes time, it goes smoother with support from loved ones. Healing was gradual. I remember awaking one morning and hearing the birds' dawn chorus.

John Julius wanted to do man's work with Jean Claude and myself of course! Mary took her tutoring duties very seriously and did not allow him to scamper off mid lesson. We all found it hard to resist John Julius's pleas, but knew it was in his interest to instil discipline at an early age.

In September 91, Mary declared John Julius' autumn term had begun. I had to laugh, but at the same time I was proud of my older sister and how seriously she took her task. Mary knew Sarah was keeping a close eye on her and Mary did not want John Julius to go away to school.

She intended to synchronize with the school terms, so that when he was older, she could align him with their syllabuses, and even take exams at the Serapeum. She had certainly done her homework. The school had a facility for children who lived too far away to attend daily and did not wish to, or could not afford to board. Mary started visiting the Serapeum library once a week to exchange books she had borrowed for John Julius. We were so fortunate with the public buildings in Alexandria, where books were available to all. A legacy from the Ptolemies, who reigned centuries ago.

Mary asked me to accompany her and John Julius, for two reasons. We did not allow the women to go to Alexandria on their own on grounds of safety, so I was their escort. I am not sure what I could have done had we run into trouble as I was unarmed and not trained in self-defence, but I was there. The other reason was to take me out of myself, for which I will be ever grateful.

Mary bumped into an old school friend, Eve, who now worked at the library. I remembered her from when we were teenagers, but being five years older, she seemed like an adult then, and I, the annoying younger brother.

She was Mary's age, 33, and had also been widowed. She came from an established Jewish Alexandrian family but wanted to remain independent - if she had returned home, her parents would have found an elderly widower for her to marry. Instead, she chose to live independently, in lodgings belonging to the library. This in itself was unusual for a Jewish woman, even in Alexandria, which was far more emancipated than Judea.

She was dark, petite and quiet in character. But I could see an inner strength which I admired and respected. I began to look forward to these weekly outings.

She was not blessed with children and took a genuine interest in John Julius, greeting him with affectionate enthusiasm, showing him the latest addition to the children's section. John Julius had turned four in June 91 and was already reading - he loved books and could often be found sitting under a palm tree reading to himself - I could see he was going to be a far better student than myself.

Eve attended the local church every Sunday in Alexandria. Mary knew I liked her and invited her to Lake Mareotis for a night, so she could see where we all lived. I was pleased it was Mary who invited her, I did not want to appear forward - it was not even a year since Helena had died. I loved Helena dearly, but I remembered her dying words urging me to look for happiness and not stay on my own. John Julius was too young to be without a mother, even though Mary considered herself that now!

Eve came after work one Friday evening and was greeted by Sarah and Jean Claude. They showed her to one of our guest cabins and she changed for evening prayers. I felt nervous, I wanted them to like her. But I needn't have worried, Sarah came to me the following day and said,

"Jude, I see you have taken a shine to Mary's friend, Eve". I blushed instantly, was it that obvious?

"Remember, no man or woman is fit to judge you. Our Lord has sent her. Eve means 'giver of life' and she will give you back yours".

I embraced Sarah. She was so wise. And she didn't miss a trick.

Our romance was a slow burner. We became friends, good friends, and on her days off, she would come to Lake Mareotis. We had both experienced grief and loss and I found her so easy to talk to - I felt like I had known her all my life (well I had actually). Neither of us had any desire to rush into another relationship. It was important she knew what her life would be like if she chose to be with me - Helena had been miserable to start with and I would not wish to inflict that experience on anyone else.

One day she asked Mother to baptize her. That was a happy day for me. Her days off turned into weekends at the community.

One year after we met, I nervously asked her to marry me, whilst we were walking along the lake shore. She took hold of both my hands and said there was nothing she would like more.

I went to meet her parents, who lived in a large house near the centre of Alexandria. I was not a great prospect in their eyes, so they were understandably underwhelmed by our betrothal. But at least she would be a respectable married woman once again and no longer their responsibility.

They insisted we were married at the local church in Alexandria. It was not our choice, we would rather have been married at Lake Mareotis; but we both felt this would be Eve's last obligation to them, and did not wish to upset them unnecessarily.

We were married by the head of the church of Alexandria, Abilius, on 7th June 93, the day after John Julius' sixth birthday. All my family attended - there was quite a procession from Lake Mareotis. We were cheered in the streets of Alexandria as we filed to the church - everyone loves a wedding. Most peoples' lives were very hard, and to share our happiness with them, even for a few moments, lifted my heart. Eve's close family and parents' friends attended, but we remained a small party. We returned to Eve's family home for a reception where Eve and I were asked many questions about the mysterious community where we would live. I could see from the puzzled looks on their faces that they did not understand the attraction, but maybe they would one day. We had chosen to focus on the inner work - for them the outer work and material world was more important. Live and let live. Tolerance for others' views would prevent many disagreements, even wars.

I was nearly 30 and much had happened since my wedding to Helena, seven years ago. This was very different. Then I had been madly in love, a giddying irrational emotional state. But I also believed my love for Eve could grow, as long as she was happy at the community. Arranged marriages were commonplace in Jewish society, and in the main were successful.

Her parents owned a summer house on one of the many islands on Lake Mareotis, so our wedding present from them was a week there. We were very excited - to have some time alone together was an unexpected treat.

Eve's father had arranged for a fishing boat to take us there. The boat was flat bottomed and propelled by a fisherman poling from the stern. It glided silently across the flat lake surface, with a gentle breeze to cool us in the afternoon sun. Fish jumped, as larger fish chased them from below. There were birds galore - ducks and geese flew overhead, cormorants dived for fish, and ibis stood in the shallows, looking regal. Ibis were a good omen. They were considered a sacred bird in ancient Egypt, associated with wisdom.

When we looked behind, we could see Lake Mareotis community on the far shore slowly receding into the distance. After an hour or so, we reached a small island with just four or five villas on it. As the boat gently beached, a short distance away, I could see an impressive white marble colonnaded villa nestling in palm trees. In front of it was a lush green garden running down to the shore line - I thought I had arrived in the Garden of Eden! We had insisted on not having servants, Eve was a good cook; the larder was stocked with greens, fruit and sprouted grains, which would more than provide for us.

It was a time to focus on one another - we did not know when there would be another opportunity. There were five bedrooms, but we chose to sleep on a day bed on the terrace, so we could retire watching the sun setting and rise at dawn. I found a mosquito net in one of the bedrooms and hung it over the daybed to save us from being eaten alive. Dawn was always my favourite time, and we were awoken each morning by a cacophony of wildlife heralding the start of yet another perfect day.

Eve had told me earlier that she was barren, as she had not conceived when she was married to her first husband, Benjamin. In Jewish society, this was considered a great failing, and usually the fault of the wife, even though no one actually knew. But I already had a son, John Julius. So bearing a child for me was not the be all and end all. It would be a gift from God, if it was meant to be. I was more interested in sharing with her what Sarah had taught Helena and I - the tantric practice.

Eve was a most conscientious and talented student - we barely left our day bed! We swam naked in the lake, as we realized we were the only ones on the island. We strolled around the island at dawn and dusk, and Eve prepared delicious food. It was a magical week.

Our time there passed in the blink of an eye - we hardly knew what day it was, but the arrival of our floating carriage after seven idyllic days and nights signified our departure from the Garden of Eden. We gathered our few belongings and were taken across the lake back to our community.

Mary and John Julius were waiting on the shore as they had seen us approaching - John Julius was in Mary's arms. I had not been parted from John Julius for a single day since he was born and my stomach lurched at the sight of him. He came rushing towards us to tell us all about his recent exploits.

Eve had been staying in Helena's cabin on her weekend visits and so it was natural for her to move into that one permanently. John Julius shared Mary's cabin, but we were all within our family compound.

And so life continued at Lake Mareotis. Eve settled in well. Although, she was Mary's friend from school, she spent a lot of time with Anne - they had a real connection. They were both academic types, real book lovers. In the mornings they would work silently in the garden before it became too hot, tending to our vegetable, herb and salad plots. Afternoons would be spent studying or copying texts in the scroll room. Eve had been trained in book binding, so ensured our codices were kept in pristine condition - they would hopefully last many lifetimes.

I started writing again... The rest of 93 was taken up writing the first tractate of Codex IX, *Melchizedek*. Mary was busy with John Julius, so Anne and Eve made copies for me, always in Greek.

Melchizedek was a high priest and king of Salem. He is mentioned in the Book of Genesis; he brings out bread and wine and blesses Abraham.

There are strong parallels between Melchizedek and Yeshua; both are called the Son of God, priest of the Order of Melchizedek, King of Righteous, King of Peace, the Messiah, appointed by God, eternal priesthood and pre-existent. In *Melchizedek*, Melchizedek *is* Yeshua - he lives, preaches, dies and is resurrected. Needless to say, Melchizedek was a greatly revered figure within our community and beyond, and this tractate proved to be a popular choice for study and discussion in the evening programme.

In the autumn of 93, Eve announced the most wonderful news - she was expecting! She had conceived during our time on the island and had waited until she was absolutely sure, some four months had passed since her last period. We were both overwhelmed and overjoyed. Eve wrote to her parents to relay the good news. As she was 35 years old, she was considered an 'older' mother, and they sent a message insisting she be attended by their doctor in Alexandria, but Eve wouldn't hear of it. Childbirth was a risky business, but we had physicians and midwives at the community. Sarah's knowledge of herbs was legendary, so we were confident all would be well, God being willing. I would regret this decision for the rest of my life.

In the small hours of 12 March 94, Eve went into labour. The baby was breach and the labour went on for hours and hours, Eve all the time losing her strength. She was attended by Sarah and Dinah, a midwife; a physician was summoned when it was clear there were complications. But they could not save Eve. They only just managed to save the baby. Mother called me in as Theodore Jude entered this world; I had to say farewell to my wife as I held my new born son - what sort of cruel twist of fate is that? Theodore means 'a gift from God'. It was impossible for me to thank God at this point. There was a hushed silence in the room. I handed my son to Sarah and stormed out of the room.

The next few weeks were a blur - I have little memory of even burying my dear wife. I could not face her parents - I left it to Sarah and Jean Claude to tell them about their daughter's death in childbirth.

Mary took charge of Theo, looking after him in Eve's cabin. Theo had dark hair framing a mid-brown face, with brown eyes as large as saucers, gazing out, completely unaware of all the grief around him... He bore a strong resemblance to his mother, which was of little comfort at that time.

Sarah's crib was once again brought out of storage, scrubbed and polished, and installed into Eve's cabin.

On his eighth day he was circumcised and when he had healed Sarah baptized him in the name of our Lord.

Losing one wife was tragic, but to lose two was too much for any man to bear. This man anyway... If it had not been for my sons I would have tied a stone around my neck and walked into Lake

Mareotis to end my anguish.

I was so consumed with grief and self-pity I barely noticed my new son. I can relate little else at that time.

Chapter X

Sarah Ascends

July 94

Life carries on, whether you wish to be part of it or not.

One summer's day, Sarah said she had something to tell me. I really had no idea what it might be, all I know is that I was not ready for what she was about to say. She said that her mother, Mary Magdalene, had come to her in a dream to tell her that she would be leaving her body in twelve months time. She was to prepare. I wheeled round in alarm,

"But Mother, surely you are not going to die, you are not even ill!" Sarah looked at me with compassion and replied,

"Jude, it is my time. I have had a wonderful life - I am 60 years old, I was born here and I will die here. I am not retiring! My work will continue in other realms..." She continued,

"I am so blessed! I have three wonderful children who are carrying on my work, and now you, Jude have given me two beautiful grandsons! It is time for me to think of the future of Lake Mareotis. I have discussed this with Mary and Anne and you should prepare to become the leader of this community, the 'One'".

She looked at me to see what my reaction would be. I had known this was my destiny all my life, but it seemed too soon, I didn't feel strong enough... Sarah was my anchor - I didn't have her organizational skills. A hundred thoughts swirled in my head. She continued,

"Mary and Anne will be standing alongside you, bringing in the Divine Feminine alongside the Divine Masculine, to make 'heaven on earth' a reality, rather than just a concept. Jean Claude will replace you as one of the 'Three'. You must continue with your writing - you have a gift and there is much more to come. As I wrote in the *Secret*

Book of James,

"They will become enlightened through me, by my faith, and through another that is better than mine. I wish mine to be the lesser."

I smiled in resigned acceptance, I knew her well enough to know this was not up for discussion.

Over the coming months, a light grew around Sarah as she seemed to become more ethereal, less of this world. Her physical energy slowly waned, and Jean Claude watched her like a hawk, barely leaving her side. Sarah would jokingly reprimand him for fussing over her, but they were quietly revelling in each other's presence, for whatever time she had left. When she felt strong enough, they would go for walks along the lake shore. Jean Claude had made two wooden armchairs, which he put outside the community hall, so Sarah sat there and enjoyed the view over Lake Mareotis.

In the early mornings, she would meditate on the Sun. This was heliotherapy. The solar rays do not stop at the surface of the body, but penetrate our bodies through the solar plexus, bathing the body and the nervous system in the radiation of the Sun. This point is the oldest unity in the human organism.

She stopped eating, food anyway. When we encouraged her to join us, she would wave her hands dismissively, saying food was not necessary for survival. She would quote the words of Yeshua,

"I have food to eat of which you do not know" referring to nourishment from the cosmic granaries.

She would watch the wildlife for hours, with a beatific expression on her face. On occasion, she would beckon one of us to come and chat with her for a while. We waited to be called - only John Julius could join her uninvited.

She spent a lot of time with John Julius, explaining the stars and planets and how we are affected by them, just as Philo had explained to her when she was his age. He helped her collect herbs and make concoctions for simple ailments, just as she had done with her mother, Mary Magdalene. He was just seven years old but never tired of Sarah's company. Sadly, her energy restricted their time together...

When she was tired and confined to her bed, one of us would give her wiki massage, a form of deep tissue massage which helped relieve her aches and pains.

We tended to her as befitted a queen; it was our turn to look after her, and this we did full of gratitude.

Sarah made Mary, Anne and I keepers of the three copies of the codices; we were not to disclose their whereabouts, and when it was time for us to leave our bodies, we would pass them onto our chosen successors. We had, and probably always would have, enemies who would happily burn our writings if not our very selves... Yeshua had foretold they would be buried for a long time and only rediscovered when humanity was desperately in need of the information, and at a time when humanity was able to receive the information.

For those with eyes to see and had ears to hear...

On the 3rd July 95, I awoke before dawn and felt called to go to Sarah. I slipped my robe over my head, and on entering her cabin was not surprised to find Jean Claude sat by Sarah's bed, holding her hand, whispering the Lord's prayer. Mary, John Julius and Anne appeared simultaneously at the doorway. There was a light around Sarah's head, and as she opened her eyes to see us all standing around her bed, her characteristic smile appeared on her face. She slowly closed her eyes as her breathing became slow and erratic, until her last breath labouredly left her body. Jean Claude kissed her tenderly on her lips and almost whispered,

"Goodbye, my love, your work is done, it is time for the angels to make you one of their own. They are lucky to have you." Jean Claude tenderly removed her wooden cross from around her neck. Peter had made it for her when she was a child. It was her most prized possession. He handed it to me saying, "Sarah asked me to give you this - she will always be with you and it will give you strength in times of difficulty."

Tears rolled down my face. She was 61 years old and still radiated such beauty... I couldn't have asked for a better mother. I placed her hands in the prayer position over her heart and kissed her on her forehead.

"Goodbye for now, Mother. Thank you for everything. I will miss you..."

As is customary in Jewish culture, we left her body in her cabin for twenty four hours, so the community could visit her and pay their respects. Jean Claude and I solemnly dug a grave close to Helena and Eve's - we buried her on the 4th July 95.

Mary and Anne wrapped her body in a white cotton sheet; the following morning before dawn, Jean Claude and I carried her on a bier out of her cabin into the garden. We gently lowered her body into the grave. Led by Jean Claude, we each threw a handful of earth onto her body, whilst I recited prayers. When the community had dispersed, Jean Claude and I shovelled the displaced earth into the grave, levelling the ground with our sandaled feet. Jean Claude had made a cross which he placed on her grave.

Sarah du Bois. Beloved wife of Jean Claude, mother to Mary, Anne and Jude, and grandmother to John Julius and Theo. 14th September 33 - 3rd July 95

Sarah left a gaping hole in the community. I missed her as our leader, but missed her much more as a mother and grandmother - she had always been there for all of us. Her love and guidance, support, wisdom, level-headedness...

I was deep in thought, skimming stones from the lake shore one day, when John Julius sidled alongside me. He turned to me and said,

"Grandma would not want you to be sad, Father. She told me her body was old and tired, and now she will be flying with the angels day and night - imagine how much fun that would be?" His eyes were ablaze with excitement and wonder.

Out of the mouths of babes... Once again, my eight year old son had put me straight... I should be happy for her rather than feeling sorry for myself. I turned to him and smiled, thanking him for his wisdom.

"Thank you John Julius for reminding me to be happy for her, instead of wallowing in my own self-pity." John Julius nodded at me approvingly - he had been understood. I remember as a child there was nothing more frustrating than when adults just didn't *get it*! I was certainly learning more from my children than I could teach them.

I still missed her, but the realization that I was missing her for my own needs prompted me to think positively. Our inner landscape determines our reality - we are in control of that. A positive outlook can make a world of difference to even the most dire circumstances.

I had not written for some months now, and I remembered Mother's words about how I must continue. I prayed to Mother that evening, and that same night I awoke in the early hours with ideas swirling around my head. Sleep was not an option. I got up, lit a candle, and started *The Thought of Norea*, which would become the second tractate of Codex IX.

It is a four paragraph ode to *Norea*, wife-sister of Seth, conceived as a manifestation of Sophia*, the 'fallen' divine Wisdom, who will be restored along with her spiritual progeny into the divine world, by the very aeons from which she once departed. She exemplifies the journey of the soul to acquire the divine knowledge necessary for salvation.

I stress the innocence of Sophia, so that her restoration to the Light no longer requires repentance for her unintentional but arrogant generation of the world creator, without the aid of her

* Sophia, which means *wisdom* in Greek, was believed to be a feminine aspect of God and a divine consort of Christ.

appointed consort, as described in *The Secret Book of John.*

It only really dawned on me how much Sarah had done at the community now she wasn't here. We only seem to appreciate things when we don't have them anymore - that is why Sarah used to remind us to count our blessings at the beginning of every day - because *everything* is a blessing. If it rains, say thank you, if the sun is shining say thank you. If you are sick, have a disease, say thank you, as it gives you an opportunity to look inside and see what is out of balance.

To not present a 'wish list' in prayer, or to pray for a particular outcome, to surrender to God's will, to go with the flow rather than desperately trying to swim upstream. I was definitely still work in progress.

Clearly on a practical level, Sarah's input had wound down over the last year, she no longer worked in the herb and vegetable garden. This was now left to Anne, as Eve was not here anymore. They had loved spending time there, getting their hands in the soil, and the garden not only looked immaculate, but was abundant in its offerings. There were always volunteers if Anne needed assistance, but on the whole she preferred to work alone.

Mary was busy with John Julius, who was now eight years old. Mary had asked Sarah if she could continue to tutor John Julius at Lake Mareotis, and not send him away to the Serapeum school in Alexandria. Sarah and John Julius had a special connection; Sarah thought John Julius was mature beyond his years, and put the question to him. He already took his studies seriously and understood the school in Alexandria was a tremendous opportunity, only available to a few. He answered without any hesitation that he considered the best option was to weekly board. He would spend Monday to Thursday in school and spend the weekends home at the community.

Mary did not voice her disappointment but it was written all over her face. She suspected that John Julius had been influenced by Sarah - they had spent a lot of time together and it was possible, but not likely. Sarah never did anything out of self-interest. John Julius had also lost his mother, step-mother and grandmother in the space of four years - he had had to grow up sooner than I would have liked.

I heartily supported John Julius in his decision - he had seen too much grief in his short life and going to school would give him another perspective on life. It was not set in stone after all - we could always review the situation. There were a few teachers at the community and we could have organized a correspondence course from the school if need be.

As a parent, I was acutely aware that John Julius was not having a conventional upbringing here at the community. There was no one of his age - he was the only child, apart from his half-brother Theo, who was only a year old. So to go away to school, especially as it was his idea, seemed sensible. It had been his decision anyway.

September 95

The day was suddenly upon us when John Julius was due to start school.

Daily life at the community rolled along, with Sunday now being our Sabbath, an indication that we were starting another week. Time was of little importance to us, but if my son was to arrive on the right day in good time, we had to pay more attention.

Mary and I took him to the Serapeum school on Monday 6th September. John Julius was excited and awake well before dawn. We left at first light, and even in our donkey and cart, it took two hours to reach the school gates. We kept our goodbyes short. John Julius was met by one of the female teachers, who John Julius confidently accompanied towards the main building. He turned around for one final cheery wave and disappeared from view. I felt quite emotional seeing my son walk away, although we would be collecting him in just four days time!

It was quickly apparent when I collected John Julius on the Friday afternoon that I had missed him more than he missed us... The right way round of course. He had found his feet and applied himself to both academic and sporting pursuits in less than a week. He never stopped talking the whole way home. I had been keen to go to school as my two older sisters were there, and I was stuck at home with our dear housekeeper, Photini. But young John Julius was the eldest and had no one to follow - he was a pioneer. I was proud of my son. Helena would have been too.

Sarah would be smiling to herself I am sure. I was more than happy to admit she had been right, just for a change.

Mary moved her attentions onto Theo, who aged 18 months was running around the place fearlessly. She was such a natural with children, she was a second mother to my boys.

With John Julius in school, I returned to writing. I wrote *The Testimony of Truth*, the third and last tractate of Codex IX.

The orthodox Christian church had begun to establish criteria for church membership. Whoever confessed the creed, accepted the ritual of baptism, worshipped regularly and obeyed the clergy, was accepted as a fellow Christian. In contrast, in our gnostic communities, members were evaluated on the basis of spiritual maturity, insight, or personal holiness. It would exclude many who the church were happy to accept, enabling the orthodox church to grow rapidly in numbers and assert their authority.

The Testimony of Truth is a rallying cry, addressed to our fellow community members, both at Lake Mareotis and other communities throughout Egypt and Asia Minor, *'who understand how to listen with their spiritual ears and not with their physical ones'.*

Its purpose was to encourage its hearers to remain steadfast in their faith, warning them of the errors of both (Catholic) Christian opponents and errant splinter gnostic groups. For the orthodox Christians say 'we are Christians', but 'do not know who Christ is'.

I opposed the law, in particular the command to procreate, and outlined the contrast between the 'generation of Adam', under the law, and the 'generation of the Son of Humanity'; consisting of those who had renounced the desires of the flesh and come to know the Father of Truth.

I also opposed martyrdom, by contrasting those with knowledge and *'the foolish'*, who are willing to suffer martyrdom for the faith, under the illusion that the Father desires human sacrifice, but remain ignorant of the true nature of Christ. These same people are also criticized for focusing on a physical resurrection, not understanding that the resurrection was really something spiritual, consisting of self-knowledge.

The Testimony of Truth relates that the gnostic path is to become a *'disciple of his own mind'*, discovering that his own mind *'is the father of the truth'*. He learns what he needs to know in meditative silence. He considers himself equal to everyone, not subject to anyone's authority: *'and he is patient with everyone; he makes himself equal to everyone, and he also separates himself from them.'*

The capstone of the homily is a description of the career of the Gnostic; his requirement to renounce the world and reintegration into the realm of imperishability,

'This therefore is the true testimony: When a person comes to know himself and God, who is over the truth, that person will be saved and crowned with the unfading crown.'

Chapter XI

Pope Clement's Martyrdom

June 99

Bad news travels fast. We heard on the grapevine, but one of Pope Clement's church officers was kind enough to take the trouble to write to me. He said that since my visit in 85, Clement had followed my progress from afar.

Emperor Trajan had ordered Clement to make sacrifice to his pagan Gods or he would be sent into exile across the Sea of Pontus, near the city of Chersonesus. Clement refused, of course, and was sent to exile. Many clerics and lay people followed him: when he landed on an island he found two thousand Christians who had also been sentenced to quarry marble there. The prisoners told him they had to carry water on their shoulders for six miles, and he said to them,

"Let us all pray to our Lord Jesus Christ to open a spring of water here in this place, that he may grant us a fountain of water and we may rejoice in his goodness!"

When he had finished his prayer, looking up, he alone saw a lamb on a hill. Realising it was a sign, he went to the spot and struck the ground with his pickaxe, releasing a gushing stream of clear water. This miracle resulted in the conversion of large numbers of the local pagans and his fellow prisoners to Christianity.

In 102, Emperor Trajan heard about Clement and sent a general to take action. Finding that all the people were ready and glad to accept martyrdom, the emperor settled for one man, Clement.

Clement was tied to an anchor and thrown from a boat into the Black Sea. A great crowd stood at the water's edge, and Cornelius and Probus, Clement's disciples, asked all the people to pray that the Lord would show them the martyr's body. At once, the sea drew back three miles, and all walked out to find a small building prepared by

God in the shape of a temple, and within an ark, the body of Clement with the anchor beside him.

It is said that every year a miraculous ebbing of the sea reveals a divinely built shrine containing his bones.

As a young man who had strayed from the path, Clement had been my first mentor and spiritual guide who had a special place in my heart. I had been moved by this gentle man and his unfaltering devotion to God. He was steadfast until the end.

I would not have had the courage to do what he did, but I also remained unconvinced of the benefits of martyrdom.

My service to our Lord was through my writing, and I needed to be alive for that. Over the next five years I wrote codices X, XI and XIII. Anne and Mary made copies for me.

Marsanes was the first and only tractate of Codex X.

Marsanes, a Gnostic prophet, describes the origin of the cosmos within which there are various levels or emanations from God. *Marsanes* focuses on the nature of the soul, both individual and cosmic; the nature of the astral powers that affect the soul, and the means by which the gnostic may manipulate these powers and ascend through the levels of the universe, until they reach the highest heaven where God resides.

Marsanes offers guidance on forming and building a community. It is aimed at the practices of an entire community, rather than the enlightenment of the individual. It includes guidance for the behaviour of community members, both inside and those outside who earnestly seek the truth.

Codex XI consisted of four tractates; *The Interpretation of Knowledge, An Exposition, Allogenes* and *Hypsiphrone.*

I wrote *The Interpretation of Knowledge* in response to internal tensions within our community. I explain that Yeshua came into the world and died for the sake of the *'church of mortals'*. Now this church, the *'place of faith'*, was split and divided into factions.

We were familiar with and united against persecution from the Orthodox church and non-Christians, but internal problems were potentially more serious and could threaten our very existence. Sarah had taught me that unity was valued above all.

Some had received spiritual gifts - power to heal, prophesise and most importantly, *gnosis**; whereas others had not. Those who considered themselves spiritually advanced tended to withdraw from those who they considered unworthy, and hesitated to share their insights with them. Those who lacked spiritual inspiration envied those who spoke out in public at the evening discourse, or spoke in prophecy, taught and healed others.

I reminded them all that all believers are members of the faith, the 'body of Christ'. I recalled Paul's words,

'For just as the body is one and has many members, and all the members of the body, though many, are one body, so it is with Christ... The eye cannot say to the hand, 'I have no need of you,' nor again to the feet, 'I have no need of you.'

To those who felt inferior, lacking spiritual powers, I offered these words of encouragement,

'...do not accuse your Head (Christ) because it has made you as an eye, but a finger; and do not be jealous of what has been made an eye or a hand or a foot, but be thankful that you are not outside the body.'

And to those who have achieved gnosis, I advise the following,

'...Does someone have a prophetic gift? Share it without hesitation. Do not approach your brother with jealousy... How do you know that someone is ignorant?... You are ignorant when you

---

* Gnosis, which means 'knowledge' in Greek, is to know oneself at the deepest level, in order to understand human nature and destiny. To know God, as the self and the divine are identical.

hate them and feel superior to them.'

As Sarah had done tirelessly over the years as the 'One', I urged all members to love one another, to show humility, to work and suffer together in order to share in the true harmony.

An Exposition was intended as a text for new initiates, explaining gnostic mythology: the creation of the world and humankind, the fall of Sophia and her ultimate return into the pleroma (fullness), together with the spiritual seed. This was followed by five short texts dealing with ritual practices: anointing, baptism and the eucharist. This further prepared them for the rites they would undergo as part of their initiation.

Allogenes, which means 'stranger, referring to the spiritually mature person who becomes a 'stranger' to the world, also describes in detail the process of attaining gnosis. Messos, the initiate, at the first stage, learns of the *'power that is within you'*. *Allogenes* relates his own spiritual awakening experience,

'My soul went slack, and I fled and was very disturbed. And I turned to myself and saw the light that surrounded me and the Good that was in me, I became divine.' Allogenes receives a vision of a feminine power, Youel, who tells him,

'Since your instruction has become complete, and you have known the good that is within you, hear concerning the Triple Power those things that you will guard in great silence and great mystery...'

Allogenes considers the revelations made to him for one hundred years.

Following this, *Allogenes* has an out of body experience, and sees *'holy powers'* that offer him specific instruction,

'Allogenes, behold your blessedness...in silence, wherein you know yourself as you are, and seeking yourself, ascend to the Vitality that you will see moving. And if it is impossible for you to stand, fear

nothing, but if you wish to stand, ascend to the Existence, and you will find it standing and stilling itself... And when you receive a revelation... and you become afraid in that place, withdraw back because of the energies... And when you become perfect in that place, still yourself.'

Messos describes his response,

*'...now I was listening to these things... There was a stillness of silence within me, and I heard the blessedness whereby I knew myself as **I am**.'*

Ecstatic with his reaction, *Allogenes* decides to go further,

'I was seeking the Ineffable and Unknown God.'

But at this point the 'powers' tell *Allogenes* to cease in his futile attempt. They command him to write down what he has learned and to place it on a mountain, under guard, with an oracle. *Allogenes* dedicates the work to Messos,

'These are the things that were disclosed to me.'

The purpose of *Allogenes* is to teach that one can come to know oneself and the *'one who exists within'*, but one cannot attain knowledge of the Unknown God. Any attempt to do so *'hinders the effortlessness which is within you'*. Gnosis involves recognizing the limits of human knowledge and experience,

'Whoever sees God as he is in every respect... or would say that he is something like gnosis, has sinned against him... because he did not know God.'

We can only come to know God through his son, Yeshua.

In summary, *Allogenes* records specific techniques of initiation for attaining that self-knowledge which is knowledge of the divine power within.

Trimorphic Protennoia was the first of two tractates of Codex XIII - the second one was *On the Origin of the World*, written by Mary Magdalene in 34, a duplicate of tractate 5 from Codex II.

Trimorphic Protennoia (Three Forms of First Thought), celebrates the feminine powers of Thought, Intelligence and Foresight.

First, Protennoia is the divine but as yet inarticulate Voice of the Invisible Spirit's First Thought. She presides over the heavenly realms for her members, and descends into the realm of chaos to give shape to her 'members', fragments of her spirit that have fallen into the world.

The text opens with the voice of a divine figure,

'I am Protennoia, the Thought that dwells in the Light... she who exists before the All... I move in every creature... I am the Invisible One within the All.

I am perception and knowledge, uttering a Voice by means of Thought. I am the real Voice. I cry out in everyone, and they know that a seed dwells within.'

Second, Protennoia is the articulate Speech of the Thought who descends to overthrow the old aeon ruled by the evil powers and empower her fallen members to prepare for the coming new age by giving them spirit or breath.

The second section, spoken by a second divine figure, opens with the words, *I am the Voice... It is I who speak within every creature... Now I have come a second time in the likeness of a female, and have spoken with them... I have revealed myself in the Thought of the likeness of my masculinity.'*

Third, *Protennoia* is the fully articulate Word, or Logos, of the Thought who descends in the likeness of successively lower powers and, entering the 'tents' of her members, conferring upon them the saving baptismal rite of the Five Seals, by which they are immersed in divine 'living water', washing away their bodily nature, so along with Yeshua, they are raptured into the Light:

'I proclaimed the ineffable Seals to them so that I might abide in them and they also might abide in me.'

Trimorphic Protennoia was my last transmission in 101, 15 years after my first writing in Antioch in 86. It was time for the next generation to take up the baton.

From 33-34, my grandmother Mary Magdalene wrote codices II, III and IV.

From 73-75, my mother Sarah wrote Codex I. From 82-84 she wrote Codex V. From 84-101, Anne, Mary and I wrote Codices VI - XIII, eight codices comprising 25 tractates.

So, over the space of 70 years, three generations of our family had written 46 tractates in 13 codices. This was Mary Magdalene's legacy and these writings were more precious to us than life itself.

It took me a long time to realize that my writing was my devotional practice to God, that only when I was writing, did I have absolutely no doubt about his existence.

The fear, insecurity and inner torture I had fought with all my life calmed and I was at peace. Writing was when I felt no fear and had faith in whatever words flowed through me.

The strength and courage I always felt I lacked roared inside like a lion ready to fight to the death.

LIST OF NAG HAMMADI CODICES

CODEX I (also known as the Jung Codex)
The Prayer of the Apostle Paul
The Secret Book of James
The Gospel of Truth
The Treatise on the Resurrection The Tripartite Tractate

CODEX II
The Secret Book of John
The Gospel of Thomas
The Gospel of Philip
The Hypostasis of the Archons
On the Origin of the World
The Exegesis of the Soul
The Book of Thomas

CODEX III
The Secret Book of John
Holy Book of the Great Invisible Spirit (The Gospel of the Egyptians)
Eugnostos the Blessed
The Sophia of Jesus Christ
The Dialogue of the Saviour

CODEX IV
The Secret Book of John
Holy Book of the Great Invisible Spirit (The Gospel of the Egyptians)

CODEX V
Eugnostos the Blessed
The Revelation of Paul
The First Revelation of James
The Second Revelation of James
The Revelation of Adam
The Gospel of Judas

CODEX VI
The Acts of Peter and the Twelve Apostles
Thunder, Perfect Mind
Authoritative Teaching
The Concept of our Great Power
Excerpt from Plato's Republic
The Discourse on the Eighth and Ninth
The Prayer of Thanksgiving
Asclepius 21-29

CODEX VII
The Paraphrase of Shem
The Second Treatise of the Great Seth
The Revelation of Peter
The Teachings of Silvanus
The Three Steles of Seth

CODEX VIII
Zostrianos
The Letter of Peter to Philip

CODEX IX
Melchizedek
The Thought of Norea
The Testimony of Truth

CODEX X
Marsanes

CODEX XI
The Interpretation of Knowledge
An Exposition
Allogenes
Hypsiphrone

CODEX XII
The Sentences of Sextus
The Gospel of Truth
Fragments

CODEX XIII
Trimorphic Protennoia
On the Origin of the World

NB: Those highlighted in bold were written by Jude

Jude's other writings:-

The Shepherd of Hermas	Rome 86
The Didache or The Teachings of the Twelve Apostles	Antioch 86
Letter of Jude	Lake Mareotis 89-90
Prologue to the Gospel of John	Lake Mareotis 89-90

PART 2 : THE LIFE OF JOHN JULIUS

Great Grandson of Jesus and Mary Magdalene

Chapter XII

Marriage, Martyrdom and New Life

July 105

Jean Claude's death blew my plans out of the water.

My grandfather died on my 18th birthday, one month before I graduated from the Serapeum. It was a shock; he was 74, but had always been fit and healthy. Except why am I surprised? Everyone in my life I am close to dies; my mother, step-mother, grandmother, and now grandfather. Like my father and grandfather, I was following in the family trade, carpentry. That was what I loved doing... I was going to apprentice with Jean Claude, but now it was impossible.

I asked my father Jude if he would train me but he said he was too busy, running the community and writing. Jude's calling was writing, but it was not mine.

In fact I had no idea what I wanted to do with my life. I knew what I was *expected* to do, to continue living at the community, and be groomed to succeed my father Jude as the 'One'...

Looking back I was probably depressed.

Jude said he understood how I felt. I looked at him quizzically. He then proceeded to share tales of his wild youthful days in Alexandria, and the real reason he had gone travelling for two years. This was all new to me. I was stunned. I was also angry. Jude was trying to help but I was unreachable at that time. Was it wrong to want a taste of freedom?

Jude came to me shortly after and suggested I wrote to Bishop Polycarp, who he had appointed as my Godfather when I was born in Antioch. He said he would love to send me to Smyrna to spend time with him, but with the relentless persecution and slaughter of Christians under the Roman emperor Trajan, it was not safe for me to travel to Asia Minor.

He did not need to remind me I was the next male heir of Mary Magdalene and Yeshua.

So writing a letter to a godfather I had met once when I was a baby, and who had had no contact with since, was my only option. I am no wordsmith, and it took many attempts to find the right words to express my feelings. Feelings had not been encouraged at the community, so it was like trying to speak a foreign language.

Fortunately, I had an ear for languages.

I poured my heart out to him - anger and grief mainly. It actually helped to organize the hundreds of thoughts swirling around my head. Before I sent it, I showed it to Jude. He sat under a palm tree to read it; he knew it was important to me. When he came to the end of the letter he buried his face in his hands, shaking his head. When he finally looked up at me, I saw tears trickling down his face. I had not seen him cry since my step-mother Eve died in child birth ten years ago. He looked up at me imploringly,

"My dear, dear son... I had absolutely no idea you were going through such torment. You have seen so much death in your short life and I was not there for you. I was so swamped by my own grief I even leant on you when you were just a boy. I hope you can find it in your heart to forgive me!" Jude stood up, looking wretched. I went to embrace him.

"It wasn't easy for either of us and I know you were doing your best..." I stopped there. As always, I felt like I was comforting him, but at least I had been heard.

Bishop Polycarp replied within weeks, although I wasn't waiting for it.

Writing my letter to him started my healing. All our answers are inside ourselves - but sometimes there is such a din coming from the mind, that we can't hear them.

It was a beautifully crafted heart felt letter, full of his love for Christ, and surprisingly, love for me. He said not a day went by when he did not pray for me. He spoke of his time with the apostle John and Mother Mary, my great great grandmother. His words touched me to my core and I felt loved. I kept his letter for the rest of my life. I turned to it when the doubts crept in, which they do for each and every one of us, including him. He said I would become a fine leader and travel to foreign lands in the fullness of time. He said he would visit me, but not yet...

I settled back into life at the community. Life was the same, but different. My outlook had changed; I slowly became aware of a bigger picture that was out of my hands, and that was where trust and faith came in. All I could do was put one foot in front of the other, live in the moment, and pray. Simple but not always easy.

Thank God for Elena. We met at the Serapeum. I had a first class education, but I always say she was the best thing to come out of it. She was far stronger than I and I clung to her like a drowning sailor in a storm. I was the weird, poor Jewish boy, who didn't fit in with my wealthy Greek Alexandrian peers, but for some strange reason, she was intrigued by me.

I knew she was special the moment I set eyes on her. Two years younger than me, she first entered my world in the school library when I was 16 and she 14. She was always cheerful, smiling from the inside out, like she had an inner light which never went out. She had long light brown silky hair, streaked by the sun.

But it was her beautiful, crystal-clear grey eyes that twinkled when she smiled, darting here and there, that I was transfixed by. She was not silly or giggly like a lot of the girls, she took her studies seriously, and never seemed to be unkind to anyone. Her name was very similar to my mother's, Helena, with only one letter different - I do not believe in coincidences.

I never thought she would be interested in me - *all* the boys were interested in her. Having no sisters, I was not familiar with the fairer sex, but my heart urged me to make conversation with her. I doubt

I made any sense - she later said I was so nervous, stuttering and mumbling. She found it most charming and refreshing, compared to the confident local wealthy boys.

I finally plucked up the courage to ask her to meet me after school. Friday was the best option, as I boarded Monday through Thursday. I arranged for Jude to collect me later - as long as we were back at the community before nightfall, which was not until late in the summer months, this was not a problem.

Our first 'date' was to the local zoo, located in the palace grounds, which I knew like the back of my hand. In my efforts to impress her, I proceeded to give her a lecture on zoology, but she still wanted to meet me again.

As we got to know one another, I relaxed and felt so at ease. We would talk or sometimes not. We walked for miles - the Paneium Park, close to the city centre, was our favourite haunt. One of the two heights in Alexandria (the other was the Serapeum), it was in the shape of a fir cone. The path to the summit was via a spiral road from where we could see the whole city and beyond. We sat on the grass under the trees, cooled by a fresh sea breeze. Above us, blackbirds, turtledoves, swallows and all kinds of musical birds sang together in harmony. It was magical.

Elena wanted to hear about life at our community at Lake Mareotis. I explained as best I could, but said one really had to experience it for oneself, as it did not make sense in the logical, material world. One could not learn to swim without getting into the water, and in the same way, one could not learn about God from reading philosophy books.

When Elena joined senior school, we were able to go out in the weekday evenings and attend classical plays at the theatre in Alexandria, go to art galleries or observe politicians working the local crowds. My peers would frequent the races at the hippodrome, betting amongst themselves, or attending their fathers' clubs for an evening's banqueting, but that was not to my taste. Nor Elena fortunately.

There was one small problem with our love match. Elena was from a wealthy, Greek Alexandrian Christian family. The relationship between the Greeks and the Jews here was fragile at best; the Greeks considered Alexandria their city, and saw the significant Jewish population as uninvited guests. There was no way Elena's family would approve of our relationship. I prayed to God for divine assistance.

Elena took a more direct approach. She was not remotely afraid of her parents. She told them she had fallen in love with a good, honest, Jewish boy, and that it was serious. They voiced their concerns, hoping our relationship would 'blow over', as most teenage romances do.

During her studies, Elena had come across the Greek poet, Sappho, who lived from 630-570 BC. She became obsessed with her work and often read it out loud to me. Born into an aristocratic family, Sappho grew up on the Greek island Lesbos, and wrote over 10,000 lines of poetry. Sappho was one of the canon of nine lyric poets esteemed by scholars of Hellenistic Alexandria. Sappho got married and had a daughter, Cleis, but this did not preclude her from having lesbian* affairs - she became most famous for her homoerotic poetry. There was a legend that she threw herself off a cliff for the love of a ferryman from a Greek island. True or false, Sappho had certainly lived life to the full.

My great grandmother, Mary Magdalene would have approved of Sappho...

And so any negativity from Elena's parents was met with a veiled threat to throw herself off the top of Pharos Lighthouse, or possibly worse, have a relationship with a woman, which as far as her family was concerned, would be more shameful than being associated with a penniless Jew.

Elena studied Judaism, so she could understand my family's history and culture. When she graduated from school at 18, she came to visit Lake Mareotis, and never left. She studied the gnostic gospels, eagerly discussing them at length with Mary, Anne and myself. Mary

* The word lesbian originates from Sappho's birthplace, Lesbos, Greece.

and Anne approved of Elena, which was important to me. Nothing would have stopped me asking her to marry me, but life was simpler with one's family onside.

I asked her for her hand in marriage as we walked along the lake shore - she threw her head back and turned to me saying,

"Nothing would make me happier, my love!" I embraced her and then we kissed. I slipped a silver ring on her wedding ring finger as a sign of our betrothal. In Jewish law, when you are betrothed you are effectively married. The custom was for the betrothal to be a year to give the bride's family time to prepare for the wedding, but there was nothing to prepare and we couldn't wait to be married.

When I shared our news with Jude, he congratulated us and said it was time for me to become a member of the 'Three' alongside Mary and Anne.

Undoubtedly an honour, but an engagement present with a difference.

June 108

We were married in a registry office in Alexandria. My father, Jude, had given me Helena's wedding ring to give Elena and I felt she was there with us in spirit. I was 21 and Elena 19. Elena's parents had the courtesy to attend - I would not understand how they felt until I had daughters of my own.

My father, Jude, arranged for us to honeymoon in a summer house on one of the Lake Mareotis islands, similar to one he and my stepmother Eve had spent a week in after their wedding in 93.

We were young, in love, in idyllic surroundings - it was all we had dreamt of. We had waited for this for so long it was almost surreal. We knew it was our week together sleeping in the same bed and we did not waste a moment. It was the happiest week of my life.

The week passed in a flash and we returned to the community via boat. Elena was assigned her cabin - hers was the seventh cabin in our family compound. Seven is a very powerful number in numerology. I felt this was a good omen.

September 108: Ignatius' Martyrdom

Jude came to see me with a letter he had received from Ignatius' great friend Bishop Polycarp. He handed me the letter for me to read. His eyes were red and swollen; Ignatius had married my parents and baptized me. He often quoted and talked of Ignatius - he had a very high regard for him.

Ignatius had stepped down as bishop in 99, but continued to be active in church life. Ignatius had for a long time prayed for the peace of the Church, fearing the danger of persecution not for himself, but for weak Christians. When Emperor Trajan returned from a victorious campaign in the East, he threatened all Christians with death. Ignatius went out to meet him and openly declared he was a Christian. Trajan ordered Ignatius to be arrested by the authorities and taken by a military guard of ten soldiers to face trial in Rome. It was unusual not to be punished locally, but Trajan wished to make a spectacle of it.

During the journey from Antioch to Rome, Ignatius and his entourage of soldiers made a number of stops in Asia Minor. Along the route Ignatius wrote six letters to the churches in the region and one to his friend Polycarp, bishop of Smyrna. Ignatius' great love and admiration for Polycarp shines through in his letter to him.

Ignatius recorded his own arrest and journey to Rome to face trial,

"From Syria even to Rome I fight with wild beasts, by land and sea, by night and day, being bound amidst ten leopards, a company of soldiers, who only grow worse when they are kindly treated." *

When he arrived in Rome and was brought before Trajan, the emperor asked him,

*Ignatius to the Romans, 5.

"Ignatius, why do you stir up rebellion in Antioch? Why do you try to convert my people to Christianity?" Ignatius answered,

"Would I convert you, too, so you would possess the highest principate of all!" Trajan shook his head,

"Offer sacrifice to my gods and you will be the chief of all the priests!" Ignatius responded,

"Neither will I sacrifice to your gods nor aspire to your high rank. Whatever you wish to do to me, do it! You will not change me at all!" Trajan then issued orders,

"Beat him about the shoulder with leaded scourges! Tear at his sides with nails and rub his wounds with sharp stones!" Ignatius remained steadfast. Trajan cried,

"Bring live coals and make him walk barefoot over them!" Ignatius replied,

"Neither fiery flames nor boiling water will quench the love of Christ in me!" Trajan responded,

"It's the devil's magic work that you can suffer so much and not give in!" Ignatius replied,

"We Christians have nothing to do with sorcery, and our law condemns sorcerers to death, but you who worship idols, you are the sorcerers!" Trajan carried on,

"Tear open his back and pour salt in his wounds!" Ignatius replied,

"The sufferings of this time are nothing compared with the glory to come!" Trajan ordered,

"Take him away and bind him to a stake! Keep him in the dungeon, let him go without food or drink for three days, and then throw him to the beasts to be devoured!"

Three days later the emperor, the Senate and the whole city gathered to witness Ignatius in combat with the wild beasts and Trajan announced,

"Since Ignatius is so stubborn, bind him and release two lions, so there won't be any remains left of him!" Ignatius spoke to the crowds,

"Men of Rome, know that my labours will not go unrewarded, and I suffer these pains for loyalty to my duty. I am the wheat of Christ! May I be ground fine by the teeth of the beasts, that I may be made a clean bread!" When Trajan heard these words, he said,

"Great is the patience of the Christians! Where is the Greek who would bear so much for his God?" Ignatius continued,

"It is not by my own strength that I endure all this, but by the help of Christ!" He then proceeded to provoke the lions. Two savage lions leapt upon him, but they only smothered him, not inflicting any wounds. Seeing this, Trajan was amazed; he promptly left the scene with orders that anyone who wanted to remove the body should be allowed to do so.

His remains were collected by his companions and taken back to Antioch where he was buried in a grave outside the entrance to the Church of St Peter.

Trajan received letters in which Pliny the Younger expressed high esteem for the Christians Trajan had put to death; Trajan regretted his treatment of Ignatius and ordered that Christians should no longer be sought out for punishment.

Jude stood there shaking his head,

"Ignatius' lived up to his name until the very end - it means 'being afire with love for God'. At least some good came out of his death..."

"Father, he was an old man - his life on earth was coming to an end and he did not die in vain. His actions will have saved many

Christians from a similar fate." Jude was not a great advocate for martyrdom, but in this case even he could not say Ignatius had suffered a pointless martyrdom.

∽

On 22nd March 109 Elena gave birth to our daughter Myriam. As Elena held her in her arms, I gazed at her iridescent blue eyes, my eyes, full of wonder and curiosity. Her head was covered with a down of dark brown hair with a distinctive reddish tint. She was our little miracle. My head was in the clouds - it was the happiest moment of my life. There is no moment to match the birth of your first born - the whole world seems to shrink, and it is impossible to focus on anything beyond this small perfect human being who has arrived straight from heaven.

This was fortunate because as an Aries baby, she would cry with all her might for attention - it was astounding how much noise, such a small person could make! Mars babies believe they are in charge, and fortunately Elena understood this instinctively. She would calmly and quietly go along with her demands, restraining her only when completely necessary. Discipline would be necessary, but only when she was old enough to understand.

Myriam walked at ten months and started talking shortly after. She was fearless, accident prone, forever covered in bumps and bruises. The terrible twos were something to behold with her fiery Mars nature. Her temper quickly rose to the fore when she was thwarted, but her anger never lasted long. After one of her frequent explosions, she would beam one of her large, bright and winning smiles and our hearts simply melted. She was demonstrative and affectionate, and wanted to please us. Her round chubby face was now framed with dark brown curls - she was simply adorable.

We learned very early on not to give her orders, to seek her cooperation firmly. She loved books - particularly stories about brave, shining heroes conquering exciting new worlds. But she also believed in the nature spirits, fairies and angels. She had a vivid imagination, and spent hours playing make believe games on her own.

Myriam was delighted at the arrival of a baby sister, Matilda, on 30th September 111. I had no desire to produce a son, even though I was the eldest great grandson of Yeshua and Mary Magdalene. It was the bloodline that was more important. Elena had given me two healthy daughters and I was the happiest man alive.

Matilda was a pink, plump angel, with a perfect bow-shaped mouth and a dimple in her chin. She lay in her crib contentedly, gazing up at us with her deep brown eyes. Myriam, aged two and a half, took charge.

Elena was not over-protective, and let Myriam carry Matilda around under her arm like a doll. She would bring her back to Elena to be fed or changed, but there was always someone around to ensure they did not venture to the lake alone.

Elena had learned to fight her battles with Myriam. She did not want to crush her young, idealistic spirit. Of course, Matilda adored Myriam. She would jerk or tremble at the sound of a loud noise - she needed peace, quiet and rest in large doses, and Myriam would rock her in little arms to sleep, before laying her gently in her crib, or sing gently in her ear to calm her. We were so happy.

But we also lived in turbulent times - there was great unrest in the outside world between the Jewish people and the Romans. Alexandria was becoming an increasingly dangerous place.

Chapter XIII

War and End of an Era

115-117: Kitos War (Second Jewish Revolt)

Figure 6: Map of Roman Empire in 117

The Jewish rebellions erupted in the year 115, when the majority of the Roman armies were far away, fighting Emperor Trajan's Parthian War on the eastern border of the Roman Empire.

A revolt in the far off province of Cyrenaica* soon spread to neighbouring Egypt and then Cyprus, inciting revolt in Judea. A widespread uprising centred at Lydda in Judea, threatened grain supplies from Egypt to the front. The Jewish insurrection swiftly spread to the recently conquered provinces. Cities with substantial Jewish populations; Nisibis, Edessa, Seleucia, joined the rebellion and slaughtered their small Roman garrisons.

*Cyrenaica is the eastern coastal region of Libya.

In Cyrenaica, the rebels were led by one Lukuas, who called himself 'king'. His group destroyed many temples, including those to Hecate, Jupiter, Apollo, Artemis and Isis, as well as the civil structures that were symbols of Rome, including the Caesareum, the basilica and the public baths.

Lukuas and his rebels slayed 220,000 Romans and Greeks. They would cook their flesh, make belts out of their entrails, anoint themselves with their blood, and wear their skins for clothing. Many they sawed in two, from the head downwards. Some were given to wild beasts and others forced to fight as gladiators.

Similar violent acts were committed in both Egypt and Cyprus. In Cyprus a Jewish band, under a leader called Artemion, took control of the island. The Cypriot Jews massacred 240,000 Cypriot Greeks, many of them civilians. A Roman army was dispatched to Cyprus, soon reconquering the capital. After the revolt had been fully defeated, laws were created forbidding any Jews to live on the island.

Lukuas led the rebels toward Alexandria, entered the city and set fire to it. The city had been abandoned by the Roman prefect, Marcus Rutilus Lupus. The Egyptian temples and the tomb of Pompey were destroyed. The Jewish rebels moved onto Hermopolis, where they prevailed in a battle in 116.

Emperor Trajan sent new troops under the new prefect Marcius Turbo, but Egypt and Cyrenaica were not pacified until autumn 117.

The Jewish rebellions were finally crushed by Roman legionary forces, chiefly by the Roman general Lusius Quietus, whose name gave the conflict its title 'Kitos'. Some areas were so decimated that new colonies had to be established by Hadrian to prevent their total depopulation.

The Jewish leader, Lukuas, fled to Judea. The Roman prefect, Marcius Turbo, pursued him and sentenced to death the brothers Julian and Pappus, who had been key leaders in the rebellion.

Lusius Quietus, the conqueror of the Jews of Mesopotamia, was now in command of the Roman army in Judea, and laid siege to Lydda, where the Jews had gathered under the leadership of Julian and Pappus. Lydda was taken and many of the rebellious Jews were executed, including Julian and Pappus.

Lusius Quietus, whom the Emperor Trajan had held in high regard and who had served Rome so well, was quietly stripped of his command once Hadrian had secured the Imperial title of Emperor. He was murdered in unknown circumstances in the summer of 118.

The situation in Judea remained tense for the Romans, who were obliged under Hadrian to permanently move the prestigious Legio VI *Ferrata* into Caesarea Maritima in Judea to maintain a fragile peace.

Farewell to Jude
9th August 124

We had celebrated Jude's 61st birthday the evening before, which was a Saturday. It was a wonderful evening - we had sung and danced well into the small hours.

Myriam and Matilda, aged 15 and 13, were growing into beautiful women, and made a real fuss of their grandfather. They flattered him, telling him how good for his age he was - Jude always responded to flattery. Vanity was his Achilles heel.

His Leo-like mane of hair and beard were now steely grey, but he was still a good looking man; he walked straight and proud, with the glide of a big cat. He was on tremendous form - enjoying being the centre of attention. He was a good host; he could make us feel like we were being entertained in a palace, even though we lived very simply. It was his generosity of spirit - his heart was made of pure gold.

It could not have been easy being on his own for all these years, since Eve died 30 years ago giving birth to Theo. Life for him without being loved was like the sun forgetting to shine... He exuded true grace and dignity, and carried his misfortunes with courage. I was seven when Eve died, and he became a loyal friend as well as a father.

There was absolutely no inkling of him being ill. It was Mary who found him. Jude did not appear for morning prayers so she knew there was something wrong. She went to his cabin and found him in bed - he looked asleep, although there was no colour in his face. She said he was still warm to the touch, so she went running for help. One of the resident physicians came quickly. The doctor said there was nothing he could do - he had had a massive heart attack. By the look on his face, Jude had died painlessly which was a comfort. I reached around the back of his limp, lifeless neck, to untie the worn leather thong bearing the cross he had inherited from my grandmother Sarah. This, together with his diary, stored in a strong box in the community grounds, was my inheritance.

Shock waves reverberated through the community. Jude had been our leader, the 'One' for almost thirty years, since my grandmother Sarah died in 95.

Jude had been steadfast, good in a crisis, never shirked his duty, held a lifelong commitment to help the defenceless, protect the frightened and cheer the melancholic. He accumulated only so he could distribute to others. He could be a just but powerful opponent, creative, original, strong and vital. He did not have a malicious bone in his body.

He had confided in me years ago tales of his errant youthful ways, the real reason for him leaving Alexandria for two years. This was not public knowledge; Sarah had kept this from the community members as she thought it would not be good for morale.

His doubts about living at Lake Mareotis reared their head again when Sarah asked him to be the 'One'; fear that he may not live up to her standards, fail, or be ridiculed for his style of leadership. His composure belied a constant inner torture masked by his natural exuberance. But once he committed to the cause, his inner strength and courage enabled him to rise to the challenge and he was fearless.

My daughters, Myriam and Matilda, were devastated. Tears flowed for days... Elena's parents never visited us at Lake Mareotis - contact was a few short visits a year to their home in Alexandria, so Jude was effectively their only grandparent. And what a grandfather he was - they were his shadows... He always had time for them, and taught them to work with wood just as he had taught me when I was a boy. Maybe he was making up for me not being able to apprentice as a cabinet maker. It would stand them in good stead in the future.

As was our custom, we left Jude's body in his cabin for 24 hours. Everyone had an opportunity to pay their respects and pray for his soul. We buried him the following day in our cemetery, next to his mother Sarah. I made the cross and Myriam wrote the inscription. After we had interred his body, I planted the cross, securing it firmly in his grave so it would not be disturbed by wild animals.

We prayed for ourselves too, to give our new leader, strength and courage in his new role. This would be me. As his eldest son, Jude had asked me several years ago to succeed him in the event of his death. The stark reality of the enormity of the role had crept up on me - I had had no time to prepare for it and did not feel ready. I smiled to myself - like father like son. Jude had felt the same when Sarah had asked him to be her successor.

My appointment as the 'One' left a vacancy in the 'Three'. It was for Mary and Anne, the other two members of the 'Three', to propose a candidate which would be voted for by the 'Council of Twelve'.

My younger half-brother, Theo, who was now 30, was the obvious choice. It needed to be approved by the 'Council of Twelve', but in all likelihood this was just a formality.

Theo was a typical Piscean fish. He was a dreamy, artistic, sensitive individual who had learned to be self-sufficient and exist on bread and water alone. His had never known his mother, Eve, so he was under no illusion about the harsh reality of life, but remained philosophical and true to his esoteric principles.

Theo had no desire to find a wife. He also had no worldly ambition

- wealth and status were an enigma to him, and his heart was free of greed. Apart from his time at the Serapeum, he had not been away from our community and had no wish to do so. He was mature beyond his years, full of deep wisdom and compassion for his fellow human beings. People flocked to him because he was non-judgemental. You could trust him with your darkest secret and be safe.

His health had never been robust, and his deep concern for others was at times a serious drain on his health. He learned his physical limitations - when his body needed rest for extended periods. But not just his body. His soul needed to be alone, so fresh breezes could blow through and heal the wounds of his and other people's troubles. But he had a hidden inner resistance. His tendency to despondency was countered by his quick-witted, satirical sense of humour.

He was a wise choice which would ensure the future of our community.

It was the end of an era when first, Anne, went to the light in October 132, and then, Mary five months later in March 133. Together in life, together in the light. They were both in their mid-seventies and had faithfully served our Lord at Lake Mareotis for over 50 years.

Mary had been like a mother to me, taking me under her wing when my mother died when I was three, and then tutoring me until I went to school at the Serapeum when I was eight.

They knew it was their time and made us promise not to grieve for them - they felt they had had wonderful lives. Simple but not easy, full of love and inner riches.

They had been nowhere and everywhere, travelling to every corner of the universe on their inner travels. Now it was time to go there and not return.

As their health declined, they prepared Myriam and Matilda to take over from them in the 'Three' alongside their uncle Theo.

Life continued at Lake Mareotis very much as before. Visitors brought news of continued discord between the Jews, Romans and Greeks, so life outside remained uncertain.

War could erupt at any time and inevitably did.

Chapter XIV

Bar-Kokhba Jewish Revolt 132-136

The Bar Kokhba revolt was the third and final rebellion of the Jews of the Roman province of Judea against the Roman Empire. It was led by Simon bar Kokhba.

The revolt was a result of continuing religious and political tensions in Judea following the Kitos war. These tensions related to the establishment of a large Roman presence in Judea, changes in administrative life and the economy, together with the outbreak and suppression of Jewish revolts from Mesopotamia to Libya and Cyrenaica.

The spark that set alight the rebellion was the construction of a new city, *Aelia Capitolina,* over the ruins of Jerusalem, and the erection of a temple to Jupiter on the Temple Mount.

The Roman prefect of Judea, Quintus Rufus, had anti-Jewish sympathies and failed to subdue the unrest early on, allowing violence to escalate and the catastrophic loss of life over the next four years.

Despite the arrival of significant Roman reinforcements from Syria, Egypt and Arabia, initial rebel victories over the Romans enabled the rebels to establish an independent state over most parts of Judea Province for two years. Bar Kokhba took the title of Nasi or *prince.* As the commander of the revolt, Simon Bar Kokhba was regarded by many Jews as the Messiah, who would restore their national independence.

The Roman Emperor Hadrian assembled a large-scale Roman force from across the Empire, which invaded Judea in 134 under the command of General Sextus Julius Severus. The Roman army was made of six full legions* with auxiliaries and elements from up to six additional legions. This huge armed Roman force finally managed to crush the revolt.

---

* A legion contained between 4,000 - 6,000 soldiers

After losing many of their strongholds, Bar Kokhba and the remnants of his army withdrew to the fortress of Betar, located in the Judean highlands seven miles southwest of Jerusalem. It came under siege in the summer of 135, and held out for three and a half years, before it finally fell. The fortress was breached and destroyed on the fast of Tisha B'av*, a day of mourning for the destruction of the First and Second Jewish Temple.

Bar Kokhba murdered his maternal uncle, Rabbi Elazar, falsely accusing him of collaborating with the enemy. Shortly after, Bar Kokhba was killed by a snake bite. The Rabbis believed Elazar's murder forfeited Bar Kokhba's divine protection. His head was presented to Emperor Hadrian after the siege of Betar.

The horrendous scene after the city's capture could only be described as a massacre. Rabbinic literature relates that the Romans, "went on killing until their horses were submerged in blood to their nostrils."

The Romans executed eight leading members of the Sanhedrin** in agonizing, heinous ways. Rabbi Akiva was flayed with iron combs, Rabbi Ismael had the skin of his head pulled off slowly, and Rabbi Hanania was burned at a stake, with wet wool held by a Torah scroll wrapped around his body in order to prolong death.

Following the fall of Betar, the Roman forces went on a rampage of eliminating all Jewish villages in the region and seeking out refugees.

The Bar Kokhba revolt resulted in the extensive depopulation of Judean communities which could only be described as genocide. Over 580,000 Jews perished in the war, and 50 fortified towns and 985 villages were razed to the ground. Many more died of hunger and disease. In addition, many Judean war captives were sold into slavery.

However, the Jewish population remained strong in other parts of Palestine, thriving in Galilee, Golan, Bet Shean Valley and the eastern, southern and western edges of Judea.

* Tisha B'Av: an annual fast day in Judaism, on which a number of disasters occurred in Jewish history; primarily the destruction of Solomon's Temple in 587 BC and the Second Temple in Jerusalem in 70 by the Roman Empire.
** Sanhedrin - an assembly of 23 or 71 elders, appointed to sit as a tribunal in every city in the ancient land of Israel.

Jewish Christians were killed and suffered all kinds of persecutions at the hands of rebel Jews when they refused to help Bar Kokhba against the Roman troops. The revolt was led by the Judean Pharisees, with other Jewish and non- Jewish factions also playing a role.

After the suppression of the revolt, Emperor Hadrian's proclamations sought to root out Jewish nationalism in Judea, which he saw as the cause of the repeated rebellions. He prohibited Torah* law and the Hebrew calendar, and executed Judaic scholars. The sacred scrolls of Judaism were ceremonially burned on the Temple Mount. At the Temple Mount sanctuary, he installed two statues, one of Jupiter and another of himself.

In an attempt to erase any memory of Judea or Ancient Israel, he wiped the name off the map and replaced it with *Syria Palaestina*. This was welcomed by the Greek inhabitants of Palestine, who were delighted at the defeat of the Jews by the Romans.

By destroying the association of Jews with Judea and forbidding the practice of Jewish faith, Hadrian aimed to root out a nation that had inflicted heavy casualties on the Roman Empire. Jerusalem was re-established as the Roman pagan polis of *Aelia Capitolina*, with Jews forbidden to enter, except on the day of Tisha B'Av.

At this time, there were many competing Jewish sects in the Holy Land; the most powerful being the Pharisees, Sadducees and Zealots, as well as the less influential Essenes.

The Bar Kokhba revolt became one of the key events to differentiate Christianity from Judaism. What set Christians apart from Jews was their faith in Christ as the resurrected messiah. Christians worshipped just one ultimate Messiah, whereas Judaism revered multiple messiahs. The two most important were Messiah ben Joseph and the traditional Messiah ben David. Christ's failure to establish an independent Israel, and his death at the hands of the Romans, caused many Jews to reject him as the messiah. Jews at that time were expecting a military leader as a messiah, such as Bar Kokhba. But Bar Kokhba had also failed to deliver.

*Torah: the first five books of the 24 books of the Tanakh or Hebrew Bible.

The disastrous end of the revolt resulted in major changes to Jewish religious thought. The Jewish belief in the advent of a messiah became abstract and spiritualized, and rabbinical thought became deeply cautious and conservative.

Jewish opinion was divided, with a large section of the Rabbinic establishment opposing Simeon be Kosiba's, also known as Bar Kokhba's, 'Son of the Star's' Messianic claims and use of violence.

Although Jewish Christians regarded Christ as the messiah and did not support Bar Kokhba, they were barred from Jerusalem along with the other Jews.

This scattered the people of Judea, leading to the Jewish exile from the Holy Land that continues to this day.

After the revolt, the Jewish religious centre shifted to the Babylonian Jewish community and its scholars. Rabbinic Judaism had already become a portable religion, centred around synagogues; the Jews themselves kept books and dispersed throughout the Roman world.

Although Judea was no longer the centre of Jewish religion, cultural and political life, many Jews continued to live there, refusing to be intimidated by the Roman authorities.

Although the revolt took place hundreds of miles away, Alexandria was not spared from the bloodbath. Over 10,000 Jews were slaughtered with the aid of Roman soldiers in Alexandria alone. In the aftermath of the rebellion, the *Sicarii** who had sought refuge in Alexandria, were put to death by the Jews themselves.

Because of the complicated three-sided relations between the Jews, the Alexandrian Greeks and the Roman rulers, the Jews vented their anger more on their unarmed Greek neighbours than on the Roman armies.

At least the upper classes stood on the side of Law and Order. But

* The Sicarii were a splinter group of the Jewish Zealots. They carried sicae, or small daggers concealed in their cloaks.

they were not safe from the mobs. Elena had tried to persuade her parents to seek refuge at Lake Mareotis - but they would not hear of it. They viewed us as some religious cult, and would rather die in their own homes than live with us. They almost did. Seventy years old and no threat to anyone, they were beaten within an inch of their lives by a teenage Jewish mob, who amused themselves by ransacking palatial homes in the Greek quarters. Their servants were slain in front of their eyes purely to inflict further pain and misery. Even Cleia the housekeeper, who had raised Elena since birth, was not spared.

A family friend wrote to Elena. Her hands shook violently as she read the letter out to me, even though they had tried to spare her all the gruesome details. Tears ran down her face from a mixture of shock and incredulity - how could they possibly do this to innocent, law-abiding citizens whose own daughter was married to a Jew?

She hurriedly gathered a few belongings and left for the city that same day. Myriam offered to accompany her but she was adamant we must stay at the community - I was the leader and both the girls were members of the 'Three'. She said she would be away for some time - as long as it took for her parents to recover.

I would visit on Sundays and we would go for a walk in our teenage haunt the Paneium, recalling happier times.

Her parents' bones were healing, but not their hearts and minds. Forgiveness for their perpetrators was beyond them - as a Jew, even I seemed to remind them of their trauma. They never said anything, but I could see a look of fear in their eyes.

Elena was deeply affected by their experience. She was quieter, less carefree, no longer the gay and lively companion I once knew. She sought refuge in the Library escaping to the world of her first love - Sappho.

Sappho had awakened her restless, unpredictable spirit. Money, fame and a career had never held any interest to her - deep inside her she was searching for an ideal, unable to identify it, as her imagination knew no boundaries. Born under Gemini, her ruling planet, Mercury, called her higher and higher. The grass is always greener and the sky bluer over another ocean. She talked of nothing else, showing only a cursory interest in what was going on at Lake Mareotis.

I thought I understood her as I was also a Gemini. We share our deepest emotions with our only constant companion, our twin self. The air is our element and true home - we are strangers to earth. Those searching questions about the meaning of life were familiar to me, as a young man I had had serious doubts about devoting my life to a community. But as I matured, I realized it was akin to chasing one's shadow - you can never catch it... I had learned to direct my search for undiscovered continents inwards.

I also had a reluctance to put thoughts onto papyrus; my father was a gifted writer and I felt I could never match him. I saw the impermanence of our reality and 'truth'. But one thing I had learned was that spiritual truths stood the test of time and we were the gatekeepers.

Elena was seeking a total blending of the mind and spirit to rediscover the beauty of life. She did not like what she saw around her in Alexandria. She thought Sappho was the answer.

Elena nursed her parents for two months. She hired new staff, and asked the neighbours to keep an eye on them. For the first time in her life, she asked them for some money to fulfil a life-long ambition to visit Lesbos, the birthplace of her heroine, Sappho. She was 47 years old and did not wish to wait a moment longer.

In January 137, the girls and I accompanied her to the harbour to see her onto a ship bound for Lesbos. There was a vivacity and excitement about her I had not seen in years. There was no point asking her how long she would be, she did not know the answer.

Myriam was subdued and Matilda shed a few tears. I suspected Myriam was crying inside - she would rather die than show open weakness. She did not understand why Elena did not want to be with us at Lake Mareotis. Matilda shared Elena's love of poetry and her respect for other's privacy meant she would not question Elena's inner desires.

Our daughters were now 27 and 25, but it must have still felt like they were being abandoned by their mother. A feeling I knew well.

Elena could not fail to see their anguish and said she would return soon. I was not so sure.

Chapter XV

Searching for Sappho

After I watched Elena's ship disappear out of sight, I told Myriam and Matilda to return to Lake Mareotis and I would meet them later. I was on a mission. I made my way to the Library of Alexandria to learn a little more about Sappho and Lesbos, the island she came from.

Poetry was not my passion but Elena was certainly under her spell. I had decided to do some research of my own at the Library of Alexandria, where her poetry once filled nine scrolls. Sadly, it was badly damaged in the fire in 48 BC, and only two poems remained in their entirety. The rest was in fragments but it was something - I was desperately trying to get inside my wife's head to understand her fascination with Sappho. It was probably futile, but I had to at least try - I loved Elena, and I wanted her back.

We had all learnt about Sappho at school, but not in the same depth as Elena. My mother and grandmother Mary Magdalene were both remarkable women; Sappho was certainly that, as well as being the first and arguably greatest female poet. This is an entry I found in an encyclopaedia,

Sappho was the daughter of Simon and Cleis, born around 630 BC in the town of Eresus, Lesbos. She was a poet of the lyre and flourished during the 42nd Olympic games, when Alcaeus, Stesichorus and Pittacus were also living. She had three brothers called Larichus, Charaxus and Erygius. She married a very wealthy man named Cerylas who traded from the island of Andros. She bore a daughter by him called Cleis. She had three companions and friends named Atthis, Telesippa and Megara, but her relations with them earned her a shameful reputation. Her pupils were Anagora of Miletus, Gongyla of Colophon, and Eunica of Salamis. She composed nine books of lyric songs comprising over 10,000 lines of poetry. She also composed epigrams, elegiac verse, iambic poetry, and solo songs. She invented the plectrum.

Lesbos is located in the North Eastern Aegean Sea, just off the coast of Asia Minor. It is the third largest island in Greece, separated from Asia Minor by the narrow Mytilini Strait, a distance of just over three miles at its shortest point.

At the time of Sappho, Lesbos was divided into five competing cities, including Erusus in the west, and Mytilene in the east, the most powerful of the island's towns.

Figure 7: Map of Lesbos

Mytilene was founded in the late 11th century BC by the Penthilidae family who arrived from Messaly and ruled the city state for 500 years. Around 590 BC, Pittacus of Mytilene led a popular revolt which ended their rule. Sappho and her family were members of the nobility, and were forced to go into exile in Sicily for several years.

In 546 BC, the Persian king Cyrus and the islanders became Persian subjects until the Persians were defeated by the Greeks at the Battle of Salamis in 480 BC. In 79 BC it passed into Roman hands but remained Greek both in language and culturally.

Lesbos is forested and mountainous with two large peaks, Mount Lepetymnos (3,176') and Mount Olympus (3,173'), dominating its northern and central sections. The island is of volcanic origin, giving rise to several hot springs and two gulfs.

Lesbos is verdant, green, and aptly named the Emerald Island, with a great variety of flora for the island's size. Millions of olive trees cover just under half the island, as well as other varieties of fruit trees. Forests of Mediterranean pines, chestnut trees and some oaks occupy around a fifth of the island, the remainder being scrub, grassland or habitation.

According to Greek mythology, Lesbos was the patron god of the island. Emigrants from mainland Greece, mainly from Thessaly, arrived in the late Bronze Age and bequeathed it with the Aeolic dialect of the Greek language, whose written form survives in Sappho's poems.

Sappho lived during a revolutionary period of Greek history, the 'Archaic Period', an age of poetry. Trade was flourishing. Phoenician traders from the Near East were filling the markets of Greek cities with exotic goods and had brought with them an alphabet from which the Greeks forged their own writing system. The first philosophers and scientists were beginning to speculate about the nature and origin of the universe.

In the previous century the bard Homer, from the island of Chios just to the south of Lesbos, had shaped the stories of Achilles and Odysseus into the *Iliad* and the *Odyssey*.

Plato was an admirer of Sappho, calling her 'Sophe' (wise) and observed,

Some people say there are nine Muses - how foolish!

See here now, Sappho of Lesbos is the tenth.

Her songs were passed down over centuries, inspiring generations of poets, although none matched her command of metre and sensual imagery.

Up until Sappho, men were the artists, intellects and leaders. Even if a girl demonstrated extraordinary artistic skills, the future of women was limited to marriage and motherhood.

Women lived quiet and controlled lives in ancient Mediterranean culture with little access to formal education. She was probably taught basic skills in reading, writing and arithmetic, in order that when she was married off in her teens, she would run a good household, bear sons and weave clothing on a loom.

But Sappho was much more than a poet. Her works clearly indicate that women - at least from her privileged social standing - had access to a formal education that included training in choral composition, musical accomplishment and performance.

Sappho was no epic poet, rather she composed lyrics: short, sweet verses on a variety of topics from hymns to the gods, marriage songs, mini-tales of myth and legend, and even politics. Some of these 'songs' - for they were meant to be sung to the accompaniment of a lyre - were for public performances; others were private compositions.

Sappho is best known for her songs of desire, passion and love - many directed to women. The verses are deeply personal and celebrate the joys and agony of the human heart:

He seems to me equal to the gods,

that man who sits opposite you

and listens near

> *to your sweet voice*

And lovely laughter. My heart
begins to flutter in my chest.
When I look at you even for a moment
    I can no longer speak

My tongue fails and a subtle
fire races beneath my skin,
I see nothing with my eyes
    and my ears hum.

Sweat pours from me and a trembling
seizes my whole body. I am greener
than grass and it seems I am little short
of dying.

Sappho had lived in a far more exciting world than Elena had been accustomed to growing up in Alexandria. Sappho not only captured her imagination, but gave her the courage to live out her dreams. Elena yearned desperately for this world.

There is no mention of Sappho's husband in her poems, but Sappho sings of her daughter, Cleis,

I have a beautiful child whose face is like
golden flowers, my beloved Cleis...

The following poem is in reference to their forced exile to Sicily,

But for you, Cleis, I have no beautiful headband

nor do I know how to get one.

But the one in Mytiline...

...to have

...adorned

...these things of the family of Cleanax

...exile

...memories dreadfully wasted away

It is clear that Sappho feels sorrow at not being able to provide a suitable headband for her teenage daughter Cleis, as her mother had done for her in the days before Pittacus - probably *'the one in Mytiline'*. *'the family of Cleanax'* were the family of Myrsilus, whom Pittacus swore loyalty to at the expense of the nobility including Sappho's clan. Through the power of her songs, Sappho is protesting against the wrongs she felt had been done to her family.

Sappho, following the poetic traditions of Archaic Greece, tended towards floral and natural imagery to depict feminine beauty and youth. Elsewhere, she evokes images of garlands, scents and even apples to convey feminine sensuality. Hers was largely a world of beauty, caresses, whispers and desires; songs sung in the honour of the goddess Aphrodite*, and tales of mythical love.

Sappho's thoughts on love and desire extend to a reverie on a woman named Anactoria. Sappho reveals that Anactoria is gone and is missed. She compares her to Helen of Troy, considered one of the most beautiful women in the world. Sappho's lyrics are sensual, gentle, intense. But they are also powerful, as she rejects the world of masculine warfare in preference for beauty and desire:

Some say an army of horsemen, others a host of infantry,

others a fleet of ships is the most beautiful thing

on the black earth. But I say

> *it's whatever you love.*

It's perfectly easy to make this clear

to everyone. For she who surpassed

---

* Aphrodite - an ancient Greek goddess associated with love, beauty, pleasure, passion and procreation. She was linked to the Romans goddess Venus. Aphrodite was worshipped as a warrior goddess and she was also the patron goddess of prostitutes.

all in beauty - Helen - left behind

her most noble husband

and went sailing off to Troy,

giving no thought at all to her child

or dear parents, but...

love led her astray.

...for

....lightly

...reminded me now of Anactoria

who is not here.

I would rather see her lovely walk

and her bright sparkling face

than the chariots of the Lydians

or infantry in arms.

Sappho's definition of beauty - that which a person loves - privileges the individual over the community. In Sappho's unique interpretation of the story, she removes the standard figures of blame for Helen's role in the Trojan War - Paris, the Trojan prince who abducted her or, in other versions, Aphrodite who forced her to go with him. In Sappho's world, where love is all, it is Helen who decides to leave her husband and elope with Paris!

This interpretation would have resonated deeply with Elena - he empowerment of the divine feminine and the belief that 'love conquers all'. Elena had now left her own husband, on a quest to find herself. I did not like to dwell on what or who that might involve.

Sappho laments the passing of her youth, but remains pragmatic.

She reminds her audience of the myth of Tithonos, one of the few mortals to be loved by a goddess. Struck by the beauty of the young man, the goddess Eos asks Zeus to permit her to take the young man to live with her for eternity. But Eos forgets to ask that Tithonos be granted a second gift - eternal youth. So she is left with a lover she quickly finds hideous and repellent, and Tithonos is left alone, trapped in a never- ending cycle of ageing.

*My heart has become heavy, my knees

that once danced nimbly like fawns cannot carry me.

How often I lament these things - but what can be done?

No one who is human can escape old age.

They say that Dawn with arms like roses once took

Tithonus, beautiful and young, carrying him to the

ends of the earth. But in time grey old age still

found him, even though he had an immortal wife.

Fortunately Alexandrian scholars produced a critical edition of Sappho's poetry. I chanced across one compiled by Aristophanes of Byzantium (c257-180 BC), when he became head librarian of the Alexandrian library at the beginning of the 2nd century BC.

Mostly fragments, a mere two or three lines, they touched my inner core.

Love shook me like the mountain breeze

Rushing down on forest trees

Love

Bittersweet, irrepressible

Loosens my limbs and I tremble

* A papyrus fragment of this poem was only discovered in 2014. Many of the other fragments had been discovered on a rubbish heap in Oxyrynchus, Egypt.

Stand face to face, friend...

and unveil the grace in thine eyes

Without warning as a

whirlwind swoops on an oak

Love shakes my heart

From all the offspring of the earth

and heaven love is the most precious.

For Sappho, poetry, song and dance were a single art form. Sappho was also a priestess and had an understanding of the celestial spheres. The following fragment suggests Sappho was versant with ancient Greek astronomy,

Full shone the moon

as around the altar stood the women

Sappho and her female companions engaged in such a dance at full moon, with the altar symbolic of the cosmos. Their choreography was a circular dance representing one or more constellations. They were aware of the harmony of celestial and terrestrial spheres, and their dance celebrated this. Another fragment,

Evening Star, carrying all that was scattered by the dazzling Dawn Star.

Sappho recognised that both stars were the same celestial object (Venus) and that she was referring to the 584-day cycle of Venus. A poem composed around a century after Sappho is on a similar theme and possibly influenced by her. The cosmos is imagined to be governed by a goddess at its centre, orbited by fiery garlands (stars), one of which is the milk of the heavens. The goddess, although unnamed, is likely to be the goddess of Love, Aphrodite (Venus). Sappho made reference to the fact the moon reflects sunlight.

The history of astronomy only makes reference to men 'discovering' this, at least a half century later.

It is thought that Sappho survived into old age and Cleis lived with her until her death. In true style, just as Socrates chastised his companions for weeping as he drank the hemlock cup, Sappho berated her daughter Cleis for crying for her mother at the end,

It is not right in the house of those serving the Muses

for there to be lamenting. That would not be fitting for us.

To complain to the gods about life coming to an end, would have been ungrateful for one blessed with so many gifts. Sappho knew her songs would live on,

Although only breath, words

which I command are immortal.

It was hard to disagree - Sappho was a truly remarkable woman and wrote some of the most beautiful poems ever composed.

Figure 8: Sappho

Chapter XVI

Dark Night of the Soul

I returned to Lake Mareotis with a heavy heart. I was just beginning to understand why Elena had gone in search of Sappho - her poetry was the truest history of the human heart. Reading Sappho's poetry had touched me deeply and only intensified my love for Elena. I missed her desperately.

Elena said she would write as soon as she found some lodgings and I eagerly awaited a letter from her. But no word came. Myriam persuaded me not to pursue her - she was right of course, but every sinew in my body told me otherwise.

So I waited, and waited. It was a dark time. I couldn't hear God, or I wasn't listening, I just didn't know anything anymore. Our days were busy so I could distract my mind during the day, but not at night. I was not a good sleeper, prone to insomnia since childhood. And I seemed to need more sleep than the rest of my family.

My sleep was fitful, and every morning I awoke with a sick feeling in the pit of my stomach, with the realization that Elena had gone. At night, my subconscious fears reared their ugly heads in nightmares featuring Elena in passionate throes with a lover, a man, or a woman, or both.

My mind told me it was not surprising Elena was not satisfied with her life here at Lake Mareotis. I had not appreciated her enough. My mother, Helena, had been desperately unhappy here... Mary and Anne had been here since they were young, and chosen not to marry, so it was different for them.

I was angry with God. I needed some time alone, away from Lake Mareotis - I was not fit to be the 'One' anyway, and I asked Theo to stand in for me.

February 137

I told Myriam and Matilda one morning before prayers that I was going in to the desert. They looked shocked and concerned, but knew trying to dissuade me would be futile.

Myriam rushed back to my cabin and reappeared with my old leather satchel my father Jude had left to me.

"Here, father, take this. You will need a blanket to keep you warm at night and a water pouch you can fill from streams!" I smiled at her as I took it - she was right - February was our coldest month, and the nights would be cold.

Matilda ran to the kitchen and returned with a loaf of bread wrapped in linen,

"Here father, please take this, at least you will eat today!' she pleaded. I shook my head, saying,

'No, Matilda, I will be fasting - but thank you'. She looked crestfallen as I refused her offering. My daughters are both determined young women and she was not taking no for an answer.

"Take it! Someone else might have need of it!" Matilda said as she thrust her bread laden hand towards me. I was not in the mood for arguing so I reluctantly put it in my bag. I embraced them both before I turned and walked towards the gate.

I looked behind once, and they were still standing there, watching me leave. Myriam stood erect and tall with her arms beside her side, and Matilda waved half- heartedly, as I disappeared from view.

I headed west along the shore line towards the desert. I felt a sense of liberation as I strode out, but it was short lived. My inner turmoil was so great I had had no concern for my daughters, who now had no idea where either of their parents were.

My mind also pointed out I was neglecting my duties at Lake Mareotis, 'not setting a good example' to the community members, running away from my problems, instead of praying. My father, Jude would never have done this. He would have stayed and prayed. But I had tried praying. It wasn't working...

Yeshua had felt driven by the spirit into the desert after being baptised by John the Baptist. He remained there for 40 days without food, living amongst wild beasts and ministered to by the angels. At the end of his time Satan tempted him three times, but Yeshua remained steadfast. The devil then left him for another time. Yeshua won that battle, but he would have been the first to point out there would be many more battles to be fought, and we can all succumb to temptation.

I walked all day long, following the sun in its sweeping arc towards the western horizon. We were in our short rainy season and what little vegetation there was was so green. I never saw another soul. Not even a bandit. Not that I wished to. There were wild beasts in Egypt; snakes, jackals, wolves, hyenas, baboons, lions and cheetahs. The Nile was home to hippos and crocodiles, but I was a long way from there. I was not afraid of them. I was more afraid of myself. At least they could put me out of my misery, so they would probably leave me alone. A cosmic joke?

Like a bear searching for a den to hibernate in, I was looking for a cave to seek refuge in. My grandmother, Mary Magdalene had lived in a cave in Gaul for 20 years or so, out of choice. There is something primal about a cave, where our ancestors lived. Mother Earth's womb - maybe I would find solace there.

Alexandria was in the Nile Delta, so the landscape was flat scrubland and desert, interspersed with sandstone outcrops and ridges up to a hundred feet high or so. Dusk came and I had not found a cave, so I slept amongst a few large boulders which sheltered me from the cool night breeze. I wrapped myself in the blanket Myriam had given me and curled up in the foetal position. I heard animal noises in the distance, but they were a long way off and didn't come my way.

I arose at first light and stretched my stiff limbs. I took a sip of water from my pouch. I was grateful to my daughters and prayed thanks to God for them. As I started walking, I realized that was the first time since Elena had left that I had actually thanked God for something, instead of hailing him with a constant barrage of requests. They say praying is talking to God and meditating is listening - clearly I needed to listen more.

A few hours passed and thought I heard a trickling of water. Maybe it was my imagination, but being the rainy season, possible. I followed the sound to find a gurgling stream, with crystal clear, ankle deep water. I was overjoyed to be able to wash my face and refill my water pouch. I sat by the stream for some time, mesmerized by watching the water happily going with the flow, either around, or over the rocks, effortlessly. Nature is so clever, being without mind. Our minds love to get involved and complicate things.

I followed the stream towards its source until it was a bare trickle. Yeshua may have been ministered to by the angels, but my faith was shamefully low, and I thought it wise to stay near a source of fresh water. I looked up and spied a craggy outcrop, with a small sandstone recess, a mini cave. There was barely room for one person and I could not stand up inside, but I was not planning on entertaining. I peered inside to ensure it was not already claimed, before entering and trying it out for size. I cast my bag against the wall.

I had collected bits of dry wood on my way together with a couple of flint stones - Jude had taught me at an early age how to light a fire. But I would wait until dark as I wanted to conserve my modest supply of dry brush.

I sat on a rock at the entrance to my new home and looked around. I closed my eyes and prayed to God for guidance, at least a sign. I sat there but I had a monkey mind. A hundred thoughts were running around my head at lightning speed.

How can silence be so deafening? I felt frustration and anger rising up inside myself. Exactly how I was feeling at Lake Mareotis - why did

I expect it to be any different here? I had changed my surroundings, but it doesn't work like that... to change the outer landscape you have to change the inner one...I knew the theory, but that is not enough. You can't experience God through theory. I was having a spiritual crisis and I needed help.

I didn't fancy my chances of a good night's sleep. My nerves were frayed and I already felt on the verge of complete nervous exhaustion - a few nights here could push me over the edge into insanity... Or maybe my resistance needed to be broken down, so I could surrender to God's will, whatever that was. I wasn't sure why I came - an overwhelming urge to escape... But one's problems have a habit of following you around, so now I had no idea why I was here. Even within my torment I could see this was my mind in supreme control over my soul.

My school teachers had chastised me for being a fidget, for having a firefly mind pursuing a thousand fancies. A day-dreamer. But there was organization in my apparent chaos. I was trying to sort, discard and decide which ideas to treasure. Why do most teachers focus on our 'weaknesses'? Always making suggestions as to how we can improve. Good teachers focus on our gifts. I hope I applied this with my parenting. Not to criticize our children, as you can so easily crush their spirit.

Elena knew exactly what education at the Serapeum was like and did not want our daughters to go there. They were tutored at the community. I am so pleased I supported her in this - they had both turned into resourceful, resilient, independent young women. I couldn't have asked for more. I was so blessed.

They were fine - I was the problem. I was also told at school I lacked persistence and patience. An impatient fidget does not sound ideal for life in a meditative community... Maybe I should try something else. But what? I was almost 50 years old and the only skills I had were home taught amateur carpentry.

It was dusk - thank goodness - time to light a fire, a practical activity. I placed a small pile of brush at the entrance to my den and retrieved the flint stones from my bag. After several attempts at rubbing the flints stones together, a small flame flickered. I blew gently at the base and was rewarded by a crackling and fizzing sound. I sat on my rock and stared at the fire - I was mesmerized. It brought me back into the present and I lost track of time. I put more brush on and decided to lie down. I felt tired and thought if sleep called, I should not ignore it.

What followed was an experience I would neither recommend nor wish to repeat. Even as I write these words, it sends a shiver down my spine. I slept fitfully, with a raging fever, sweating, then icy chills, tremors... I heard myself shouting, yet it failed to rescue me from this marathon nightmare.

My overriding memory was sheer terror, and a desperate feeling of being alone, falling, falling into a dark black abyss full of writhing serpents, hissing and projecting their forked tongues towards me from below. I had always had a fear of snakes... I kept falling, falling, desperately reaching out for something to grasp hold of.

I felt an icy chill which penetrated my very core. Ghouls, spirits, demons, with distorted freakish faces surrounding me, some without mouths, huge, black eyes, making a deafening screeching sound, yet at the same time hauntingly laughing at me. I would have opted for death at this point to end my torture.

It seemed to go on for an eternity - I was paralysed with fear and for the longest time I couldn't cry out. I don't know why it took me so long to ask for help - maybe I had to go through my own dark night of the soul to heal my wounds. Then I saw a glimmer of light coming towards me, and I felt hope. I was not alone. We never are. Something inside me, my soul, enabled me to cry out in desperation to Yeshua, the angels, God - anyone who could help me. Please, please, anything but this.

And then I heard a choir of angels, faintly at first, but gradually getting louder and nearer. I was blinded by a light brighter than that of a thousand suns. There was a feeling of being loved and peace beyond all understanding. There are no words to describe it. I had never felt this before in my entire life. It was like I imagined heaven to be when I was a small child. It was so real... If I never experience it again I will die a happy man, as I now know where I will be returning to.

Then I saw Yeshua's face, smiling at me, with both his arms extended towards me. He took me in his arms and I cried like a child, all the tears I didn't shed when my mother died, the tears I didn't shed when Elena left for Lesbos, burst out in an uncontrollable torrent in this moment.

The fear had subsided - I was being held, by the angels, and I felt safe and loved to my core, probably for the first time in my life.

Then I heard a voice, gentle but strong, soft but firm,

"John Julius, it is time for you to spread your wings and await the New Jerusalem, which will come down from Heaven from God, as foretold by John in *Revelation.*"

"But where?" I asked, puzzled.

"On top of a mountain, in a deserted place, far away. You will be guided by angels. Take your daughters with you. Have faith." Then I awoke. I had no idea how long my nightmare or visions had gone on for - I looked up and the sun was already high in the sky, so some time. The fire embers were stone cold. My mouth was parched so it could well have been more than one night.

I heard a gentle cooing and I looked down to see a small white dove sat beside me, cocking her head to one side as she studied me, her eyes darting around, surveying my den. I remembered the bread Matilda had given me and I slowly reached for my bag, trying not to frighten the bird. I broke off a piece, which was rock hard by now, crushed it into large crumbs and scattered it in front of me. She eagerly pecked at the pieces and I watched, transfixed. My mind stilled, as time slowed down and I enjoyed the company of my new friend.

I recognized the dove as a sign of the Holy Spirit; a dove appeared above Yeshua after he was baptized by John the Baptist. I felt a sense of peace I had not enjoyed in a long time, if ever. There are signs around us all the time, if we keep our eyes and ears open.

I thought about the terrifying nightmares I had had. Sleep had enabled me to bypass my mind and delve into my core wounding, the sense of abandonment I had felt at the two most important women in my life 'deserting' me - awareness is the first step to healing. I felt blessed. One can turn one's traumas into gifts, a form of alchemy, for the benefit of oneself, but also for others.

My dove had had her fill and flew off. I wondered if I would see her again. It came to me there is no such thing as a farewell, as separation is an illusion. And you should set free what you love most - if it flies away and returns, it is meant to be. True love. Yeshua tried to teach us this. I closed my eyes and settled into my body - I could feel every cell, my monkey mind was not in control for once. Information without energy is knowledge, not wisdom. I intended to integrate this experience, however long it took. Patience, acceptance and trust was in order. If I stayed with the feeling, there would be a shift - if it took 40 days so be it. This was an opportunity not to be missed - I had faced my demons - they were part of me - I could not ignore them for the rest of my life. I had never thought of befriending them, treating that part of myself with love and compassion, instead of pushing them away.

I was brought out of my reverie by a gentle cooing sound - my new friend was back. She had returned for her evening meal. It was almost dusk, but instead of springing into action to light my night fire, I took some more bread out of my bag and placed a few crumbs in the palm of my hand. The dove did not hesitate to hop onto my palm, trusting its new food source as a friend rather than foe. Her pecking tickled me, and I tried to keep still and not giggle. But the more you try not to laugh, the harder it is to suppress it, and I found myself laughing out loud until my stomach ached. I could not remember the last time I laughed like this! The dove was unperturbed, finished the crumbs and flew off.

I did not light a fire, I felt safe and protected by a warm inner glow. I happily retreated to my den, wrapped myself in my blanket and fell asleep instantly. I dreamt of my life from childhood to now, like a series of pictures in rapid succession. From my earliest memories, cutting wood with my father, Jude, my mother reading to me.

My times at school, courting Elena, our marriage and birth of our daughters. And Elena leaving for Lesbos... The images in my head were accompanied by a myriad of emotions - love, joy, but anger, fear and panic too. I felt it rising uncontrollably. Then I saw my mother's face - I had forgotten what she looked like, but there was no mistaking her. She looked at me, her face full of love and compassion... There were no words, but I felt a strong sense of regret for the hurt she had caused by leaving father and I. Father said she had never been really happy at Lake Mareotis. I realized her soul had wanted to go home, but she had stayed with us as long as her soul could bear.

Then an image of Elena flashed into my head, and my mother looked at her, and then at me with the same expression. She did not want Elena to suffer the way she had and if I truly loved her, I needed to completely let her go.

I awoke once again to cooing. She was back. It was the start of another day. All we can do is put one foot in front of the other and keep going. Life is not easy, but there are loved ones to support us, both in this world and the next.

I emptied the rest of the bread from my bag and packed my blanket and water pouch into my bag. I made my way to the nearby stream to refill my water pouch to slake my thirst and sustain me on my homeward journey.

It was time to return to the real world, or my real world anyway,

Lake Mareotis. I felt a sense of excitement and zest for the next chapter of my life.

God had plans for me, I was all ears.

Chapter XVII

Theo's Initiation

The lookout guard spotted me and sent word to Myriam and Matilda of my return. They came running out of the compound to meet me, and I embraced them with all my heart, body and soul. It was a wonderful feeling. I thanked God for my family, with a special prayer of thanks to Elena for giving me these two beautiful young women. I had not lost Elena, we would meet again, sometime, somewhere...

"Father! You have been gone for seven days and we were so worried about you! You looked so distressed when you left, and now you look, well, refreshed... How wonderful! Tell us all about it!" They were both jumping up and down with excitement and I did not know where to begin... I raised my hand and replied calmly,

"Patience, girls, I do have a lot to tell you, but not in this very instant! I will tell you what I can remember at the evening meal, not before!" They feigned a look of disappointment, took me by the arm, and escorted me back to my cabin.

"Of course, father. Please forgive us. You should refresh yourself and change your tunic. We can wait!". They were overexcited, but it's good to be missed.

I shared my experiences at the evening discourse so all our members could hear, as far as I could remember anyway... I hoped others might benefit - it is perfectly normal and expected to experience doubts and misgivings. We are all One and sharing really helps. Showing one's vulnerability gives others permission to do the same. For me personally there had been a shift. The girls said they could see it in my face, in everything about me. I certainly felt different; much clearer, lighter of heart.

Some weeks earlier, I had received a letter from Gaius Heliodorus, the newly appointed Roman prefect of Egypt. He was related to Philo, who had been my grandmother Sarah's tutor when she was a child. He was enquiring about the character of our Christian religion, and why had I embraced it. I had started a reply, but felt unable to finish it, as I was full of self- doubt at the time. I left it on my desk.

When I returned, I noticed that the letter from Gaius had been replied to, by Theo. As far as I knew, this was his first official letter.

At that moment, Theo appeared, looking slightly apprehensive.

"Ah Theo, I see you have used your initiative and dealt with a matter I was procrastinating over." Theo looked relieved to see I was not displeased with him for replying to a letter addressed to me.

"Perhaps, you could tell me what you wrote in your reply?"

Theo explained that he had entitled his discourse *Epistle of Mathetes to Diognetus'. Mathetes* means 'disciple' and *Diognetus* was a pseudonym.

He felt it prudent not to disclose the identity of the addressee, as Gaius had written to me confidentially. Gaius had suffered the misfortune of having to deal with the aftermath of the Bar-Kokhba Revolt - he had been horrified at the brutalities that had taken place in Alexandria at the hands of Roman soldiers. He had expressed his Jewish sympathies publicly, and as a consequence, been heavily criticized and reprimanded by Emperor Hadrian. Theo did not want to add fuel to the fire. Theo wrote it anonymously, of course, although he sent it with a signed covering letter.

It was in the form of twelve short chapters, summarising why Christians abandoned Judaism and Paganism, with a description of the character and behaviour of Christians at that time.

Our beliefs are based on the teachings of Yeshua, our Saviour, who was sent by God. An extract from Chapter VII - 'The Manifestation of Christ', reads as follows,

"As a king sends his son, so sent He Him, seeking to persuade, not to compel us; for violence has no place in the character of God... As loving us He sent Him, not as judging us. Do you not see that the

more of them are punished, the greater becomes the number of the rest? This does not seem to be the work of man: this is the power of God..."

An extract from Chapter XII - *The Importance of Knowledge to True Spiritual Life,*

"When you have read and carefully listened to these things, you shall know God bestows on such a paradise of delight, presenting in yourselves a tree bearing all kinds of produce and flourishing well, being adorned with various fruits. For in this place the tree of knowledge and the tree of life have been planted; but it is not the tree of knowledge that destroys - it is disobedience that proves destructive... For neither can life exist without knowledge, nor is knowledge secure without life. The Apostle perceived that knowledge without true doctrine, declared, 'Knowledge puffeth up, but love edifieth.' For he who thinks he knows anything without true knowledge, knows nothing. But he who combines knowledge with fear, and seeks after life, plants in hope, looking for fruit. Let your heart be your wisdom; and let your life be true knowledge inwardly received... Amen.

Theo received a reply from Gaius thanking him for his educated discourse and that he had some further questions. He would like to continue correspondence with him, confidentially of course. I congratulated Theo on his letter,

"Well done Theo, this is progress - a seed has been planted for the future." Theo smiled modestly.

If I was off to new pastures, Lake Mareotis would be in good hands with Theo.

New Jerusalem

My mind kept returning to the prophecy of the 'New Jerusalem' from the angel who visited me during my 'dark night of the soul'. I studied *Revelation*, the book John the Evangelist wrote during his exile in Patmos. In particular, the section prophesising the events of the last days. Unveiled in the book are the invisible forces and spiritual powers at work both in the world and in the heavenly realms, including forces at war against the church.

Revelation starts with,

"This is a revelation from Christ, which God gave him to show his servants the events that must soon take place. He sent an angel to present this revelation to his servant John".

Revelation is a glimpse into the invisible spiritual battle in which good battles against evil. God the Father and his son, Christ, are pitted against Satan and his demons. Christ has already won the war, but in the end, he will come again to Earth. At that time, everyone will know that he is the King of Kings and Lord of the Universe. Ultimately, God and his people triumph over evil in a final victory.

The second coming of Christ is an imminent reality, so God's children must remain faithful, confident and pure, resisting temptation. Christians are cautioned to stay strong in the face of suffering, to uproot any sin that may be hindering their fellowship with God, and to live clean and undefiled. God abhors sin and his final judgment will put an end to evil. Followers of Christ will achieve salvation because Yeshua conquered death and hell.

Christians are destined for eternity, where all things will be made new. The believer will live forever with God in perfect peace and security. His eternal kingdom will be established and he will rule and reign forever victorious.

The destruction of Jerusalem and building a new city is foretold,

"Then I saw a new heaven and a new earth, for the old heaven and the old earth had disappeared. And the sea was also gone. And I saw the holy city, the new Jerusalem, coming down from God out of heaven like a bride beautifully dressed for her husband. I heard a loud shout from the throne, saying,

"Look, God's home is now among his people! He will live with them and they will be his people. God himself will be with them. He will wipe every tear from their eyes, and there will be no more death or sorrow or crying or pain. All these things are gone forever."*

"One of the seven angels said to me, 'Come, I will show you the bride, the wife of the Lamb.' And he carried me away in the Spirit to a mountain great and high, and showed me the Holy City, Jerusalem, coming down out of heaven from God. It shone with the glory of God, its brilliance was like that of a very precious jewel... It had a great, high wall with twelve gates, with twelve angels at the gates. On the gates were written the name of the twelve tribes of Israel... The wall of the city had twelve foundations, and on them were the names of the twelve apostles of the Lamb.

The city was laid out like a square, as long as it was wide. He measured the city with a gold measuring rod and found it to be 12,000 stadia[1] in length, and as wide and high as it is long. He measured its wall and it was 144 cubits[2] thick, made of jasper, and the city of pure gold..."**

"I did not see a temple in the city, because the Lord God Almighty and the Lamb are its temple. The city does not need the sun or the moon to shine on it, for the glory of God gives it light, and the Lamb is its lamp..." ***

"Then the angel showed me the river of the water of life, as clear as crystal, flowing from the throne of God and of the Lamb down the middle of the great street of the city. On each side of the river stood the tree of life, bearing twelve crops of fruit, yielding its fruit every month. And the leaves of the tree are for the healing of the nations... There will be no more night... And they will reign for ever and ever."

"Behold, I am coming soon!... Blessed are those who wash their robes, that they may have the right to the tree of life and may go through the gates into the city, Outside are the dogs, those who practise magic arts, the sexually immoral, the murderers, the idolaters and everyone who loves and practises falsehood.

*Revelation 21: 1-4   **Revelation 21: 9-18   ***Revelation 21: 22-24

[1] About 1,400 miles (about 2,200 kilometres)
[2] About 200 feet (about 65 metres)

*I, Yeshua, have sent my angel to give you this testimony for the churches. I am the Root and the Offspring of David and the bright Morning Star."**

Every cell in my body tingled with excitement as I read these words. The New Jerusalem! All I needed to know was where.

Chapter XVIII

Pepouza, Phrygia, Asia Minor

April 137

I did not have to wait long. One night an angel came to me and said it was time for me to leave for Phrygia, Asia Minor. I should take a boat to Miletus, on the west coast of Asia Minor south of Ephesus. From there, I would take a boat along the River Meander and make my way to a city in the Ulubey Canyon called Pepouza. All would be provided along the way. The angel said I should take Myriam and Matilda with me. We would found the 'New Prophecy' movement.

Myriam and Matilda were even more excited than I. They were 28 and 26 years old and had never left Lake Mareotis - aged 50 neither had I. To us all it was an adventure we were more than ready for.

All that needed to be done was to appoint our replacements to ensure the continued smooth running of our community. I proposed Theo to be the new 'One'; I was confident he would be a balanced, fair, leader. He had been born with an understanding of esoteric principles and shown an interest from an early age in astrology and numerology - he was more than capable.

Myriam and Matilda each proposed a female member of our community to take their places on the 'Three'. They were duly approved by the Council of Twelve. We boarded a trading ship in Alexandria bound for Miletus. It was a distance of over 450 miles and would take 4-5 days if we went directly and had fair winds. A few stops on route would extend our voyage to around a week.

We got chatting with the captain and he asked us where we were heading. I told him we were planning to travel up the River Meander and then onto Pepouza on foot. He asked us if we had a boatman, and when I shook my head, immediately volunteered his cousin, Marcus. Ask, and you shall receive.

The captain was proud of his birthplace, Miletus, and when he was not on watch, shared his extensive knowledge of the local history.

By the 6th century BC, the great port city of Miletus was the undisputed cradle of Western art and philosophy. Greeks had settled there from their homelands across the Aegean some centuries earlier. Home to musicians, poets, philosophers and sculptors, Miletus also boasted planners, engineers and the earliest map makers.

Miletus sat at the mouth of the Meander* Valley, famously fertile from the substantial silts carried down by the Meander river, equally rich in historical figures as it was in fruit and vegetables.

An epic cast of gods and mythical heroes, conquerors, kings, traders and travellers had trodden the ancient road that ran along much of its broad valley to connect the Aegean with the Asian hinterland. Alexander the Great, founder of Alexandria, had subdued Miletus in 334 BC before conquering much of Asia.

This route connected Miletus with India, carrying vast caravans of wool, wheat, spices, marble and ivory.

Miletus harbour was at the southern entry of a large bay, with a large marble lion the proud mark guiding ships through shallow water.

From the 5th century BC, if Miletus was to remain a port, the mainstay of its wealth, it was obliged to retreat inland. The gulf was silting up with alluvium carried by the Meander River, advancing at around 20 feet a year. The waters around Miletus were turning to mud and extensive dredging was required. The coast was being pushed further into the sea, with several small islands off the coast being united with the mainland.

The Romans made impressive civic additions to the city; a colonnaded agora, temples and a monumental baths complex. The baths complex was commissioned by Empress Faustina in the 1st century. Beneath high walls to deter prying eyes, the baths were

* The word 'meander' used to describe a winding pattern, comes from the Meander River

open to the blue sky. In the frigidarium, where bathers plunged into the cold waters of a low square pool; at the head of the pool a bearded, muscular god of the river, Meander reclined, naked except for a sheet slung loosely at his navel. Reflecting the abundance of the Meander valley, he had flowers in his hair, a horn-shaped basket in his arms, overflowing with pineapples, pomegranates, grapes and other fruits of the valley.

Miletus became an inland town in the mid-1st century. In 57, the apostle Paul met the elders of the church of Ephesus, near the end of his third missionary journey, as recorded in Acts (Acts 20:15-38). Paul stopped by the Great Harbour Monument and sat on its steps, met the Ephesian elders there, and then bade farewell on the nearby beach.

We arrived early in the morning - the sky was cobalt blue and there was not a breath of wind. The captain invited us to his home where his wife provided us with refreshment whilst Marcus and his crew were located. We would leave by noon - Marcus wanted to take advantage of an onshore breeze which got up late morning, and would aid our progress upstream. Marcus' boat was a small, flat bottomed skiff with a mainsail and a jib. We would discover later why it had to be small. He had two boatmen to raise and lower the sails, and more importantly, paddle either side with an oar. The sails would only be of use where the river was wide, and we could take advantage of the wind in our backs. As the river narrowed, paddling would be our only means of propulsion. I volunteered myself and the girls to help with the paddling. Marcus pointed to three smaller oars stored in the bow for that very use.

To begin with, the Meander River sat in a shallow, wide, flat-bottomed valley. I could feel a gentle swell coming from the Aegean Sea. As I turned around, I could see surf breaking where the sea funnelled into the river. There were fishing boats dotted around at anchor, with fishermen standing in waist deep water, silently chewing sunflower seeds, whilst casting their nets.

The area was teaming with wildlife. Near the river bank, a pat of pink flamingos standing on bamboo thin legs, were feeding on

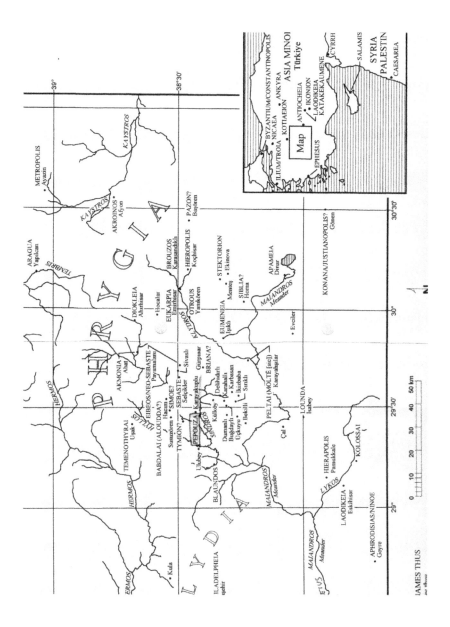

Figure 9: Map showing location of Pepouza, West Phrygia, Asia Minor (now Turkey) Pepouza was discovered by archaeologists Tabbernee & Lampe in 2000

samphire in the salt flats. Something disturbed them and they promptly all lifted in a line. A prehistoric looking grey heron glided past our boat, with a silvery fish clenched in its beak, still wriggling. White storks stood in the shallows, motionless. A drift of pochard ducks floated gently downstream, the wind ruffling their henna plumages. A procession of pelicans passed, in perfect formation, their wings in effortless unison. Directly above us, egrets trailed their legs across the sky.

The water, deep through the flatlands, was clear; the river bubbled and flashed with fish. Turtles basked on the banks, wavelets nudging their black shells, where they surfaced at the foot of the reeds. Out on the open reaches of the river, a stiff sea breeze raised the waves to little hackles.

Beyond the river banks, lay magnificent farming country. The farmlands of the Meander valley were known as the orchard of Asia Minor. Rightly so. The high productivity was a natural consequence of the rich topsoil silts that the regular winter floods deposited across the plain. The river frequently overflowed its banks, so there were no homes built within the flood plain. The Lower valley produced figs, citrus fruit, strawberries, sesame, liquorice, olives, apricots, walnuts, pomegranates, cotton and silk. The area was also famous for its wine.

In the Upper valley, wheat, cherries, apples, and capers were more common. The river was over 300 miles long from its source, near Dinar, to the sea, but with a gentle gradient, dropping less than a mile in height in its entire length. Hence, the river wound tortuously and sinuously, contorting in a continuous, flattened 'S', traversing from one bank to the other.

As we were travelling upstream, it was important that Marcus directed his oarsmen to parts of the river which offered the least resistance. Here where the river was wide, the current was gentle, but as it narrowed the current would gather momentum and this tactic would prove essential.

As we proceeded inland, an imperceptible rise in the land's lie caused the river's languid curves to tighten into bends, and its width narrowed drastically. As the valley narrowed, the rocky heights closed in on the river, obscuring our view beyond the river. The surface of the water was embroidered with sudden ruffles and swirls. We came across rapids, and had to go ashore while the crew carried the boat to a point above the rapid where we could safely get back on board.

The landscape changed dramatically, the vineyards replaced by cherry blossom orchards and Judas* trees, celebrating spring with their radiant pink flowers. Willow trees hung over the riverbanks. The woven spheres of weaver birds' nests hung from the branches. Sparrow gangs marauded around searching for bedding material.

Marcus said at some points the river was as wide as it was deep, and only small craft could navigate this part of the river. I quickly learnt that one thing all willow branches did was split and fall. These fallen branches had to be negotiated, through, around, or when they blocked our way completely, we were forced to exit the river and relaunch a little further upstream.

Reeds closed in on either side, rising green from their fronded bases, to sun-bleached crackle-dry seed heads. Above their fluffy tops, to the west, I caught sight of sunlit limestone uplands.

At dusk, swallows swooped around us to pluck the water's surface. A flock of bee eaters, yellow and red, passed low overhead. Frogs came to life from the shallows, croaking loudly to one another. In the late light, a skein of geese flew overhead, black against the pink sky.

When nightfall approached, Marcus found a suitable place where the banks were not steep and we could clamber out. Marcus tied the painter to a tree and we made our way to the nearest village seeking refuge. The locals were friendly and inquisitive - they were used to boats coming up and down the river, who provided extra income in exchange for lodging. Marcus found a local farmer, who sold us some fruit and offered us a barn for the night. We were relieved to stretch our stiff limbs, and slept soundly nestled amongst hay bales. The girls said it was all part of the adventure!

---

* The Judas tree is a small deciduous tree which grew throughout Judea. It was called Judea's tree and at some point morphed into Judas tree as a result of the myth that Judas hung himself on one.

We went through narrow valleys and canyons, with snow covered mountains majestically looming in and out of view in the distance. After living in the flat Nile Delta for many years, the scenery was breath-taking and we all sat there open- mouthed admiring God's handiwork.

On the third day, the rapids were becoming more frequent - it was clear we were reaching the upper limit of our voyage. We came to a small settlement - Marcus said he could go no further. He also told us he knew of a local travellers' inn where we could all rest for the night. From here on we would have to continue our journey on foot.

Over a delicious dinner of fried fish, I spent the evening explaining the 'New Prophecy' to our fellow travellers. My father, Jude, had said I could talk myself in and out of situations with the greatest of ease, swerving anyone from their deepest held convictions! I was also blessed with a good ear for languages, and was able to understand their local dialect, which was different from the Greek the Alexandrians spoke.

After a good night's rest, we regretfully bade farewell to Marcus and his crew. Before doing so, we invited them to join us at Pepouza. I sincerely hoped they would be able to, one day.

We set off on a well-marked path, climbing steeply, always within earshot, if not sight of the river. At times we could hear the river roar, and we were glad to be on terra firma!

The river forked, and my intuition guided me to follow the course to the right.

My gut feeling was confirmed by oncoming fellow travellers, who assured us we would be at a village called Ardabau before dusk, where we could rest for the night. Sure enough, we found an inn and were welcomed once again. Over a simple meal of bread, soup and cheese, we chatted with the locals and they asked questions about the 'New Prophecy' as we called it.

Myriam said I went into an ecstatic trance, and proclaimed the following,

"I am the Lord God, the Almighty dwelling in a human. Neither angel nor ambassador, but instead I, the Lord God, the Father, did come."

Prophetic activity thrived in the Christian church at this time. Our local audience, small as it was, seemed genuinely interested in the New Prophecy.

The following morning we bade farewell to our new friends who assured us we would reach Pepouza that day. They told us Pepouza was a vast, rich city, and could only be reached by traversing a narrow, precipitous path.

We prayed to our Lord and his angels for protection, and set off with high spirits. As we climbed, the views took my breath away! Sometimes there was a vertical drop of several hundred feet, with nothing to break a fall should we lose our footing. After climbing for most of the day, the path finally levelled. A sweeping descent was marked by wicker baskets heaped with fresh cut meadow fodder lying by the path - we were approaching civilization.

We had been kept safe, as promised, and on reaching Pepouza made our way to the local church. We sat on a pew at the back and prayed thanks to God for our protection and deliverance.

We were approached by two elders who were cleaning the church. They bade us a warm welcome and offered us refreshment, enquiring from where we came. When I explained who we were and the distance we had travelled, they immediately offered us board and lodgings, as we would have done at Lake Mareotis.

Phrygia was home to an Oriental ecstatic cult of Cybele and her male consort Attis. Cybele was the mother goddess of fertility. She was Phrygia's only goddess, and its national deity. In a Phrygian rock cut shrine, she was called 'Mother of the mountain'. She was depicted as an exotic mystery-goddess with attendant lions, a bird of prey, and a small vase for her libations or other offerings. Processions show her as arriving in a lion-drawn chariot to the accompaniment of wild music, wine and a disorderly, ecstatic following. She had a eunuch mendicant priesthood.

She was revered as a mediator between the boundaries of the known and the unknown, the civilized and the wild, the worlds of the living and the dead. Her association with hawks, lions, and the stone of the local mountainous wilderness, characterized her as mother of the land in its natural state. She had power to rule, moderate or soften its latent ferocity, and to control its potential threats to a settled, civilized life. As protector of cities, or city states, she was often shown wearing a mural crown, representing the city walls. At the same time, her power transcended any political stance and spoke directly to her followers from all walks of life.

So the local people were used to a woman being in charge. They would not be opposed to Myriam and Matilda standing alongside me and being in positions of equal authority.

The following morning I climbed to the summit of a nearby mountain, Omercali, to observe the topography of the surrounding area. Pepouza was located on the River Sindros in the Ulubey canyon; Tymion, some eight miles north, was situated on the plateau itself. Tymion was part of a Roman Imperial Estate farmed by non-slave tenant farmers.

The towns Pepouza and Tymion would now both be referred to as 'Jerusalem', marking the northern and southern limits of the area the 'New Jerusalem' would descend to out of heaven. It was a large, flat, agricultural tableland large enough to be the landing place of the new holy city. I was convinced this was the place referred to in *Revelation*.

I was overcome by the beauty of this land. The contrast between the Meander River, which had been a feast of wildlife, and now the expanse of mountainous scenery around was awe inspiring. I felt at home here already.

I decided to honour this sacred place by changing my name to Montanus, which means 'mountain'.

The Church elders invited me to preach on the following Sabbath - I did not prepare any notes - I prayed for guidance and waited to be filled with the Holy Spirit. I stood at the front of the church and explained about the New Prophesy, about how John foretold in *Revelation* how a New Jerusalem would descend from the heavens - how I had been guided to Pepouza, as this is where it was going to take place, and soon. As I started to speak, once again, I became possessed by the Holy Spirit. I went into an ecstatic trance, describing the New Prophesy.

"The righteous will shine a 100 times more than the sun, and the small ones among you who are saved will shine a 100 times more than the moon."

I was not speaking as a messenger of God but felt possessed by God and completely unable to resist. I urged the congregation to fast and pray, so that they might share my revelations, which were available to all.

We were received well by the local people, who were excited that their remote, quiet place had been chosen by God to be the new centre of the Christian faith. I was invited to speak again the following week - I was pleased to see the pews were almost full.

I was convinced that the end of the world was at hand, so I laid down a rigorous morality to purify the Christians and detach them from material desires.

This included restricting marriage to one time only, in the same way as there is only one God; arduous fasting, an emphasis on virginity, the desire for martyrdom, and a penitence regime for the forgiveness of sin.

Our teachings were a form of spiritual revival through the New Prophecy within orthodox Christianity, based upon the *Gospel of John* and *Revelation*.

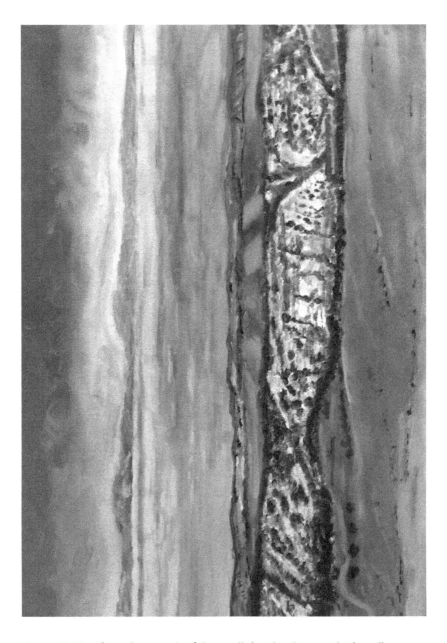

Figure 10: View from the summit of Omercali showing Pepouza in the valley and Tymion in the distance

We honoured Christian beliefs and accepted its apocalyptic, end of the world themes, but rejected the Church hierarchy uniformity of a hierarchically organized Christianity which did not allow individual religious expression.

As the church of the New Prophecy, the movement spread quickly throughout the Mediterranean basin. The success in the Phrygian hinterland was aided by the fact that rural dwellers, unlike those in the city, had fewer places to participate in the emperor cult, and so were less likely to be persecuted by the Roman authorities.

Chapter XIX

Elena Returns

June 137

An angel came to me one night and told me my patience and heart's desires would be rewarded shortly, that I should not be angry, but give thanks to God for her safe return.

It had to be the return of my wife Elena. The thought of it brought up a myriad of emotions. My heart ached for it, but feelings of hurt, anger and abandonment swirled around creating inner conflict and turmoil.

On the following Sunday, Elena strolled into our church with a huge smile on her face, as if she was returning from a trip to the market... I stood still, temporarily struck dumb by a large lump in the back of my throat. Elena came rushing towards me and threw her arms around me, exclaiming,

"John Julius, my love, I have missed you so much!"

"I am called Montanus now" I replied flatly. I was simmering with irritation and my voice was trembling with emotion. Then I remembered what the angel had said, and sighed as I took a deep breath to collect myself. This was what I wanted, right? But why hadn't she written? I had a hundred questions, but my busy mind was interrupted by the arrival of our daughters, who were clearly overjoyed to see their mother. This annoyed me too - where did their loyalties lie? Myriam and Matilda came rushing towards Elena, exclaiming,

"Mother, how wonderful! You found us! We are all together again!" The girls jumped up and down with excitement, but I felt anything but elated. Pride and anger, a toxic combination, were waiting impatiently in the wings. I took another deep breath and counted to ten. I did not want to say anything in the heat of the moment that I would regret later. I turned to her and said calmly,

"Elena, I have a few matters to attend to, the girls will show you to our lodgings - assuming you intend to stay?"

"But I have so much to tell you!" she implored, "can't they wait?" Elena knew me of old, and used her womanly guiles to good effect. She took me firmly by the arm, and announced,

"Let's go for a walk!" The girls smiled in approval - they also knew their mother would get round me, as she shared the same powers of persuasion as myself... We walked for hours, like in the old days. As she talked I realized how much I had missed her and my anger gradually subsided - if I cannot forgive my own wife who am I? She hadn't actually done anything wrong anyway...

She told me all about her time on Lesbos, what an incredible place for women it was, how she had joined various women's groups; learnt to write poetry, play the lyre, sing in a female choir and take part in all women ceremonies including full moon ceremonies. I told her I had also done some research on Sappho and my appreciation for her had grown immensely. Elena looked pleased.

She had been delighted to discover that Sappho had not thrown herself off a cliff for unrequited love of a ferryman - just a rumour perpetuated by men for men.

She had written to me at Lake Mareotis, but it arrived just after we had left. Theo wrote and told her of my plans to start a movement in Pepouza - word reached Lesbos and she assumed it was me and the girls. She had left immediately. Elena turned to me, her grey eyes sparkling with excitement, and said seriously,

"John Julius, or Montanus, if you prefer, I am sorry if I hurt you. I never stopped loving you, but I had to go to Lesbos to explore myself. There was this deep yearning in my soul that I could not ignore - I thought you of all people would understand this desire." I did understand, but I had focussed on my own needs, not hers.

"Elena, please forgive me for being so selfish. I should have trusted you. Praise our Lord for delivering you safely here - we have much work to do!" She cocked her head to one side and gave me one of her irresistible smiles - I took her in my arms and gave her a long, embrace. I could feel her heartbeat and didn't want to let her go. Her scent was so sweet...

"Montanus, this is a new beginning for us and I think I will change my name too. *Quintilla* came to me." I looked at her quizzically.

"*Quintus* in Latin means five; it is my angel number and is associated with love, marriage and divine grace. So, it represents our marriage and my love for you; divine grace brought us together and will enable us to carry out our mission here. Furthermore, I dreamt that two women would be joining us shortly, making five of us." She looked at me expectantly,

"My dear, I think Quintilla suits you very well."

"That's settled then. From this day forth I shall be called Quintilla!"

Maximilla and Priscilla

I had a dream where Yeshua's face appeared to me in the form of an androgynous man woman form. I thought of the words of Paul who said,

*"There is neither Jew nor Greek, slave nor free, male nor female, for you are all one in Christ."**

I gave it no further thought, as I had been raised in a community set up by a woman, Mary Magdalene, and then led by her daughter, Sarah, my grandmother. The New Prophecy expected the Holy Spirit to give gifts to both men and women. We were not the first; Moses' sister, Miriam and the apostle Philip's four daughters were all recorded in the scriptures as having prophetic gifts.

One day soon after, two women walked into our church with the poise and confidence of those high born. They introduced

*Galatians: 28

themselves as Maximilla and Priscilla. Little did I know then how important they would be to our mission.

Maximilla, walked tall, with her raven haired head held high, decorated with a silver headband. She had a long straight nose and olive skin - my guess was she was native to this land. Her friend, Priscilla, was smaller with curly dark brown hair and bore an uncanny resemblance to my daughter Matilda, with an engaging smile and perfect white teeth. Priscilla had had a vision,

"Having taken the form of a woman, Christ came to me in a radiant garment and placed in me wisdom and revealed to me this; this place (Pepouza) is holy and in this place Jerusalem will come down from heaven."

Priscilla shared her vision with her close friend Maximilla; they both decided they had no choice other than joining us here in Pepouza, leaving their wealthy husbands and children behind.

As my great grandmother Mary Magdalene had helped fund Yeshua's mission, Priscilla and Maximilla were happy to contribute to the running expenses of our New Prophecy movement. History was repeating itself...

Priscilla and Maximilla were in no way spiritually dependent on me - we all preached, but I also organized and promoted the movement.

Myriam and Matilda assisted me in this, just as they had done at Lake Mareotis. I appointed Theodutus as our financial officer, and Themiso as his assistant. Themiso wrote a general epistle summarizing the principles of the New Prophecy for newcomers. I was 50 years old and saw Theodutus as my successor, unless the New Jerusalem had arrived before then of course...

Belief in the Second coming of Christ was not confined to the New Prophecy movement, but our activities characterised a popular revival. The belief that the New Jerusalem would soon descend on the town of Pepouza attracted many prophets and followers, who welcomed ardent hopes of Christ's imminent return. They revelled in the austerities which diminished the terrors of persecution, and opened visions of the future reward.

The essential principle of the New Prophecy was that the *Paraclete*, or the Spirit of truth, whom Yeshua had promised in the Gospel of John, was manifesting himself to the world through my words, and also those of the New Prophecy prophets and prophetesses.

"But when he, the Spirit of truth, comes, he will guide you into all the truth... and he will tell you what is yet to come." *

My words were simply a direct revelation of God. Our followers acknowledged the religion of the New Prophecy as the pure, unadulterated Gospel, and our utterances as the voice of the Spirit.

The new Prophecy did not deny any of the church doctrines, or attack the authority of the bishops. The church acknowledged the charismatic gift of some prophets. But it soon became clear that the New Prophecy was new. True prophets did not, as we did, induce a kind of ecstatic intensity and a state of passivity, and then maintain that the words we spoke were the voice of the Spirit. I was criticized for claiming to be God, but I was not, God was simply speaking through me.

I was also claiming to have the final revelation of the Holy Spirit, implying that the teachings of Yeshua and the Apostles were incomplete.

Official criticism against our movement was aimed at our unorthodox ecstatic expression and neglect of the bishop's divinely appointed rule. Just to add salt to the wound, a further offensive to the patriarchal Church was our admission of women to positions of leadership.

We celebrated and stressed the importance of chastity or purity, being more conducive to the work of the Spirit, to harmony, visions and auditions.

*John 16:13

Our services were overlaid with customs of the local Cybele cult, as a token of our respect to the local people - it had been predominant for hundreds of years and had not felt threatened in anyway by our presence.

We had services where seven virgins dressed in white carrying torches, enter the church and deliver oracles to the congregation. This often caused a reaction of tearful repentance in members of the congregation.

These virgins, grieving for Christ's suffering, recalled the Cybele virgins who mourned the passing of Attis during their spring festival. He was a Phrygian god of vegetation. In his death and resurrection, he represented the fruits of the earth which die in winter only to rise again in the spring.

Our popularity grew and many Christian communities were almost abandoned. This gave the Orthodox Church cause for concern.

Apollinaris, Bishop of Hierapolis, convened a synod of twenty six Asiatic bishops in Hierapolis to determine what course of action they should take to contain our movement. They voted unanimously in our condemnation.

They focussed their attack on our women.

Apollinaris sent Zoticus, with his clerical aides, to exorcise the spirit of Maximilla. This was thwarted by Themiso and a few others, with Zoticus leaving in a fit of temper calling Maximilla a series of names - 'mad', a 'victim of the devil', a 'spirit of deception' and hostess to 'bastard spirits'. I swelled with pride as Maximilla retained her composure and calmly relayed to the onlookers,

"I am driven away like a wolf from the sheep. I am not a wolf, I am word and spirit and power." A loud cheer erupted from the congregation, which further incensed Zoticus and his retinue, speeding their departure.

She was making a direct reference to the words Paul had written in Corinthians. A charismatic female prophet was not expected to be well acquainted with Scripture...

Bishop Sotas of Anchialus' subsequent attempt to exorcise Priscilla was similarly prevented. Here was war: male against female; bishop against prophetess; catholicity against holiness; universalism against sect; hierarchical against Church of the Spirit. But the first count was the most important - there were no exorcisms against our male prophets.

The Catholic Church and its bishops harassed us wherever we thrived. Our prayers were answered by an unexpected visit by Bishop Polycarp of Smyrna accompanied by his assistant Marcianus. My godfather. I had had no communication with him since I wrote to him over 30 years ago.

He strode in as if he had been out for an afternoon stroll. His hair and beard were almost white, but his small wiry frame was well preserved. He belied his age - he must have been 80 years old or so, but walked unaided, and spoke with the energy and vitality of someone much younger.

"Montanus, how wonderful to make your acquaintance! You have been causing quite a stir in the area, and following my promise to you when you were just 18, thought my visit to you was somewhat overdue!" I excused myself to retrieve the letter he had written to me all those years ago. I held it in the air as I came back into the study.

"It is one of my most prized possessions and I seek counsel from it in dark times". Polycarp answered wryly,

"You would do better to seek counsel from our Lord". He then laughed out loud. I remembered my father Jude saying how much he enjoyed the company of Polycarp and Ignatius, who teased one another constantly. I liked this man. Modest, bright, without a shred of pride or arrogance. Polycarp was serious for a moment,

"I am keen to learn about your New Prophecy Movement - my fellow bishops are getting very hot under their collars and I fear for the safety of your prophetesses. I have followed your progress from afar, believe it or not, and am your godfather after all!" He burst into raucous laughter again.

Polycarp and Marcianus stayed with us for a week, attending church services with much discussion and prayer in between. On our last evening Polycarp said to me,

"As I thought, you are a true and genuine servant of our Lord. I see your father in you - well the apple doesn't fall far from the tree," as he chuckled to himself. "My fellow Catholic bishops will never accept women as their equals, even though that is what Christ preached. All I can do is continue to pray day and night for unity in all our churches throughout the world, including yours of course. I still have a little influence, but I would strongly advise you to have your prophetesses accompanied at all times - there is always a rogue wolf at bay."

I was sad to bid Polycarp farewell - we both knew we were unlikely to meet again, pity enough; there was a lot I could learn from this sage old man.

From then on Maximilla and Priscilla would be accompanied by either myself, Themiso or Aleibades, who became official leaders under Maximilla. Polycarp had modestly underestimated his influence, and there were no further attempts to exorcise Priscilla or Maximilla. They became popular leaders in their own right, with a gift of delivering oracles with a living message. Just as Mary Magdalene, Sarah, Jude and myself had done so at Lake Mareotis, as the 'One', in our evening discourses. Maximilla explained her mission,

"The Lord has commissioned me as a separatist, illuminator, and interpreter of this suffering, covenant and promise." She was proclaiming the relationship of the suffering of God's people and the preparation for God's redemptive intervention.

Priscilla's words were equally powerful,

"The holy minister knows purity in order to serve, for purification is in harmony... and they see vision, and hear distant voices as beneficial as they are hidden."

Their oracles were written down, circulated and afforded high status, to the chagrin of the Orthodox Church. And they were women. This together with their ecstatic uncontrolled state, was intolerable. They were troublesome and should be seen off.

Myriam and Matilda were spared from exorcism on account of the fact they were frequently away evangelizing, first within Phrygia, then throughout Asia Minor. I followed Polycarp's advice; I was not only their leader but also their father, and they never travelled alone, always accompanied by one of our senior members.

Quintilla was happy supporting me here in Pepouza. We were living as man and wife, but more importantly, we were united by our shared passion for the New Prophecy.

When the prophetesses were all in Pepouza, Priscilla and Matilda were inseparable, like 'two nostrils are to a nose'. They discovered they shared the same birthday, so Priscilla used to joke they were twins.

At 32, Priscilla was six years older than Matilda, but looked up to Matilda, who had had a much more emancipated upbringing at Lake Mareotis. They had much to compare...

Priscilla had been raised in luxury; educated, but with the sole expectation of marrying well, managing a household, weaving, and bearing a child, preferably a son. Matilda had been raised in a community, valued as one of our principal members, with no expectation of marriage. She had nothing materially, but was rich beyond measure, having been nourished since birth with love and community. She was confident, cheerful, and beautiful, radiating a light that no one could fail to notice.

They came from such different worlds and yet had so much in

common, brought together by our mission here in Pepouza. They talked endlessly, exchanging childhood tales - they seemed to read each other's mind, finishing one another's sentences, which sent them into further fits of laughter. It was wonderful to have such joy in our household. It was infectious and lifted all our spirits.

They certainly had a special connection - but nothing lasts for ever.

Chapter XX

Pepouza Cave Community

July 139

The locals had kindly furnished us with a small house near the church for my family to live in. The arrival of Priscilla and Maximilla meant we needed more space.

I had spotted the deserted cave complex from the summit of Omercali mountain, when I first surveyed the land around Pepouza. It was less than a mile west of the town. Quiet, but not too remote for fetching supplies.

The earliest inhabitants found shelter in the numerous large caves in the scenic Ulubey Canyon. At some places, the canyon widened to form a basin. The Pepouza settlement developed on the River Sindros in one of these basins, which widened by several hundred yards. The river was flanked by dense pinewoods and Judas trees. These would provide firewood for building materials, heating and cooking. Fresh water and land suited to agriculture made it an ideal location for a settlement.

The edge of the basin was framed by rugged perpendicular limestone walls. The cave complex was cut into the limestone rocks of the canyon's northern wall.

It was surprisingly extensive; spread over three floors, with over 60 individual cell-like caves. From the first level, a wall of over eight feet rose to the floor level of level two. To climb to the second level, we climbed steps cut in the rocks by ancient inhabitants.

As I cast my eyes around, my amateur carpenter's eye envisaged fitting wooden installations - balconies along the front of each facade to enable access to each cave from the outside, wooden doors to safeguard any valuables and keep the heat in in winter. Little did I know these would contribute to our downfall...

Figure 11: Pepouza Cave Community (2000)

Pepouza Cave Community

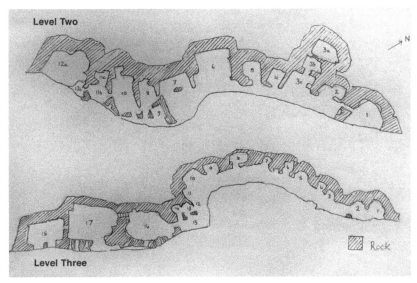

Figure 12: Pepouza Cave Community Layout

Level Two

1   Store for valuable objects

3a   Cooler room

3b   Storage room

3c   Dining room

6   Central area

10   Chapel

11a   Sleeping room

12a   Refectory

12b   Storage

Level Three

17   Baptismal pools

18   Montanus' room

Surfaces could be chiselled and smoothed, floors levelled with loam, niches cut into the rock to make benches, beds and shelves.

In the centre of level two, there was a large three sided grotto with a half-domed ceiling. On either side, there were a further fifteen caves, all connected. The large central room would serve as a reception and meeting room.

As the first level was some eight feet above the ground, we would need to install a winch rope pulley system to hoist up supplies to the upper levels.

A substantial tree trunk would be installed. An indentation would then be made in both the floor and ceiling to secure the tree trunk in a vertical position, which could be turned by a donkey as a rope winch, to lift objects from the foot of the cliff to the upper levels. This was one of the first installations we carried out, as we needed to install our tools and supplies in wooden baskets and pails.

The half domed grotto was a spacious area; one corner of the room would be set apart and partitioned as a stable for our donkey Amos, the lower part converted into a semi-circular seating area. A wooden cross would be attached to the ceiling; two long pieces at right angles joined in the shape of a cross.

The largest cave on this level would serve as a refectory. A chapel would also be located on this level.

Cooking would take place in an outer cave on the first level; a natural depression in the floor would be ideal for a fireplace and smoke could escape through two outlets in the ceiling. Our diet was simple; bread, water, fruit and vegetables. We did not eat meat or fish. We would bake bread, just as we did now, with an impression of a Eucharist ceramic bread stamp for celebrating the Eucharist.

Level three comprised 18 caves, three of which were large. Two of these would be connected by a low passage, and serve as baptismal pools. Water dripped through the ceiling from the porous limestone

Figure 13: Ceramic Bread Stamp* for making Eucharist bread

rock above and could be collected to fill the pools. Drains chiselled into the floor would enable the pools to be emptied towards the balcony.

My room would be on this level too, adjoining one of the baptism caves. I would install a wooden partition so that one half was for writing and sleeping, and the other for praying. A low step could be carved under a large niche at the rear of the cave so I could kneel to pray. Both rooms would open onto the balcony with a view across the valley.

Each level featured a series of caves which would be perfect for our purpose - our own cave community!

In honour of my great grandmother Mary Magdalene, we would install a white marble statue of her to remind us of our heritage and the sacrifices she made for us... There were two marble quarries

* Discovered by Tabbernee & Lampe in 2001, during their archaeological dig near the church remains in Pepouza

outside Pepouza - I would commission one straight away!

This would be a perfect headquarters for the New Prophecy movement; of course there was much to be done, but we had funds, expertise and many pairs of willing hands. I jotted down a few measurements, made some sketches and hurried back to Pepouza to put my plans into action - I was excited beyond belief!

We would continue to preach at the local church and beyond, but this would be home. We would also be able to accommodate visiting pilgrims. And so work began. It was summer so we could work long into the evenings. We sang hymns as we worked, everyone pitched in, happily. Practical issues arose, but were solved effortlessly - I felt God was working with us.

This was one of the most rewarding times of my life - building our very own community. Progress was swift and we were able to move in in the autumn. The locals gave us animal skins to line our stone beds and keep us warm in the winter nights. We installed supplies and moved our few belongings to our new home; Quintilla, Maximilla, Priscilla, Miryam, Matilda, Themiso, Aleibades and Theodutus, myself and twelve of our followers. Work would continue when we were there - all the communal areas, and most importantly, the chapel, were finished to a high standard and worked on with loving care.

Daily life was similar to how it was at Lake Mareotis, rising early, praying and bathing in cold water before any of our daily activities commenced.

Every morning, I would stand on the balcony outside my room and savour the view across the canyon - the best view in the whole world.

For now, numbers were such that councils were not necessary, but when they increased, we would adopt the same hierarchy we had at Lake Mareotis with the 'Three' and the 'Council of Twelve'. For now, we were intimate enough to be led by me as the 'One'.

I was content beyond measure. My women folk were fulfilled. These were happy days indeed - I mistakenly thought nothing could go wrong.

June 140 - Gaul

As a child, Myriam had loved tales of brave heroes discovering exciting new worlds. So it was little surprise when she came up with the idea of travelling to Lyons, Gaul to evangelize the region. The New Prophecy had already spread throughout Asia Minor and the Mediterranean basin - their sights were set further afield.

She had another reason to travel to Gaul - she wished to trace her roots back to where her great great grandmother Mary Magdalene fled from Egypt in 43 and was washed up on the beach at Marseille. She was accompanied by her brother Lazarus, her sister Martha, her nine year old daughter Sarah, Mother Mary, Mary Salome, Joseph of Arimathea and Maximin. Myriam wanted to see for herself if almost 100 years later, her ancestors were revered, or remembered at all...

Matilda was always keen to travel and equally enthused, but knew there was one person who would be desperately unhappy about this development - Priscilla. There was no way of cushioning the blow - Priscilla cried and begged her not to go, saying it was dangerous, foolhardy, premature - when this approach did not work she said she would go with them. Matilda said they would return but Priscilla screamed,

"You won't, I know you won't! I will never see you again! How can you abandon me?" I was relieved when Quintilla offered to intervene - I would rather face a wild beast than a hysterical woman...

We had to put the priorities of the movement first - our disciples travelled in pairs, and it was diluting our resources unnecessarily for Priscilla to go with them. Priscilla was truly heartbroken when Myriam and Matilda left. I knew how she felt - when Quintilla, or Elena as she was then, left me in Alexandria for Lesbos I felt a desperate sense of abandonment. Priscilla did little to disguise her feelings and it was raw viewing. She was inconsolable for days... even her dear friend

Maximilla could not comfort her. We prayed for her - it was all we could do.

Rome was now the intellectual centre of Christendom. Its headquarters had moved from Jerusalem to the capital of the Roman Empire. All who wished to influence the Catholic church flocked there. Themiso and Aleibades would accompany Myriam and Matilda as far as Rome to preach to the local people. It was unlikely the Bishop of Rome would wish to see them, but we left it in God's hands.

Themiso relayed to me on his return that they made their way to the Parthenon, where the local philosophers tended to congregate and air their views. The learned men argued against the likelihood of a new city descending from heaven - how could that possibly happen? So they relocated to agoras where the local people were - there was more interest here.

Myriam and Matilda took it in turns to prophesize, and the crowds grew on a daily basis. Most people were illiterate at that time, so it was futile handing out the Epistle Themiso had written - oral teachings were more powerful and trusted by the average man in the street.

They urged the crowds to make haste and travel to Pepouza, where they could prepare for the arrival of the New Jerusalem. Most people were poor and lived hard lives, with poor sanitation and not enough to eat - the idea of being provided for and being part of this exciting new movement was enticing.

As a matter of courtesy, I wrote to the Bishop of Rome, Pope Pius I, to request an audience. But our request was declined - he was keen to distance himself from our movement. We were not unduly disappointed; we were confident the seeds were sown, would germinate, and spread by air and water to all corners of the world in due course.

Themiso and Aleibades left Rome and made their way back to Pepouza, whilst Myriam and Matilda took a trading ship to Marseille.

Myriam said that when their ship sailed into the old port of Marseille, something stirred in her soul and she had a feeling of deja vu, an old memory passed down through the generations perhaps.

This is where Lazarus, older brother of Mary Magdalene, became first bishop of Marseille. He did many good works before Emperor Nero had him beheaded in May 61.

But the girls had another place nearby in mind - the fishing village Saintes Maries de la Mer, some 30 miles to the west. When Mary Magdalene retired to a cave in La Baume forest, this is where Mother Mary and Mary Salome spent the rest of their days, from 43 until their death in 56.

The two Marys took custody of my grandmother, Sarah, who was just twelve years old at the time. This was also the home town of my grandfather, Jean Claude, a cabinet maker. The locals built a church in honour of the two Marys, where Sarah and Jean Claude were married. They wanted to visit the church and see whether there was any record of their lives there.

The girls strolled along the port, watching the fishermen unload their catches.

They had no trouble persuading a young fisherman to take them to Saintes Maries de la Mer - a combination of Greek and sign language enabled them to make their request understood! The fisherman had finished for the morning, and was hardly going to miss an opportunity to have two attractive young women in his boat.

A fresh breeze in their backs enabled a smooth, fast sail along the coast to the fishing village Saintes Maries de la Mer. The fisherman Jean gently beached his boat and helped them ashore. He refused to take any payment, jumping back into his boat after wishing them good luck with a cheery wave.

The church was easy to spot. It was set back a little way from the sea, on top of a hill, to protect it from storms and flooding.

After making their way along cobbled stone streets, they entered the church through a large, wooden door. The church was in perfect condition, with a high arched wooden ceiling. They were pleasantly surprised to find the tombs of the two Marys in pride of place at the front, with the bow of a blue wooden boat jutting out from the wall. A model of the boat they had sailed over from Egypt in. Inside the boat were two effigies of the two Marys. Myriam and Matilda stood in silence, mouths open. Then Matilda rushed forward, she had spotted something else.

"Myriam, look! Sarah is here as well!"

At the front of the church was a diminutive figure, dressed in a blue cloak, with a tiara on her head. She was only four foot or so, clearly a child, with a dark skinned face.

Inscribed underneath was the name 'Sara' - there was no doubt this was in honour of their great grandmother. Myriam and Matilda sat on a nearby pew and prayed for some time.

An older woman was nearby busily arranging flowers - she had noticed them come in and been watching them out of the corner of her eye. She knew they were not locals and was curious. She approached them offering them a glass of water as there was a spring inside the church. Not only was there living water for baptisms, but the church had often provided shelter for those with no place to go. She put her hand gently on Myriam's arm as she said,

"It is not very comfortable, but you are welcome to stay - it is warm, dry and I can bring you some food?"

"Oh, that would be most welcome, thank you!" Myriam answered. She then enquired,

"Tell me, have you heard of the du Bois family? Our great grandfather was a cabinet maker called Jean Claude du Bois and we wondered if they still lived in the village?"

"Well, of course - there is a du Bois family who live nearby - I will take you there straight away - they will be delighted to meet you!"

Myriam and Matilda stayed for two weeks with Philippe du Bois and his family. Philippe was Jean Claude's great nephew, grandson of Jean Claude's brother Philippe, and named after him.

They told Philippe and his family all about their community life at both Lake Mareotis and Pepouza. They were fascinated. It was also apparent that the two Marys and Sara were very much woven into the local fabric and folklore. The du Bois family and their friends were thrilled to host two of Mary Magdalene's great great granddaughters.

They were invited to stay as long as they wished, but Myriam and Matilda had plans to travel up the Rhone to the city of Lyons.

Many Greeks from Asia Minor had migrated there who would hopefully be receptive to the New Prophecy.

My own feeling was that Myriam and Matilda would not be returning to Pepouza anytime soon - I decided to withhold that information from Priscilla as it would only confirm her worst fears - that Myriam and Matilda would not be coming back, just as she had foretold. I would leave that thorny task to Quintilla.

Chapter XXI

Pepouza Church

March 141

I was very happy at our cave community, but it was not suitable for the large numbers of pilgrims, some elderly and infirm, who arrived daily in Pepouza to await the arrival of the New Jerusalem.

These people were not just the poor or oppressed. They included professionals disenchanted with their lives; physicians, teachers, stonemasons, architects and engineers. All people who felt there was something missing.

It was time to build a church that could accommodate them - we had a wealth of expertise at our disposal to enable this. Money was not a problem - people who could afford to made donations, and all gave their time on a voluntary basis.

I had grand plans to build a white marble church north of the river on the edge of Pepouza town. I had spotted a large rectangular terrace of land, with a west - east orientation, overlooking the River Sindros. Marble was an expensive material, but Pepouza was blessed with not one but two local quarries; one on the south side of the river at the eastern end of town, and a second quarry in the Ulubey Canyon further east.

This second quarry was more difficult to get to, involving a steep climb along a narrow donkey path which snaked upward through the rock and undergrowth, making dizzying switchbacks over the void.

After a rainfall, a waterfall spilled in front of the path making it slippery and treacherous under foot. But the reward was larger, more valuable slabs, justifying the risk and effort.

Both quarries were 'owned' by the Roman Emperor and part of the Tymion Estate, run by tenanted farmworkers. The Romans requisitioned anything of value. This did not bother *me* -better to be poor in the material life and rich in the eternal one, but the plight of the highly taxed estate workers living from hand to mouth, was a gross injustice which made me angry. I would try to find a way of secretly compensating the estate workers - we were a remote part of the Roman territory and not under close supervision, but we would have to be careful.

I liked to draw and had good spatial skills from my carpentry training, so I put both to good use, sketching out plans for our new church. I had discovered a talent that made my heart and soul sing - creating buildings to carry out God's work.

First the cave community and now a church. I showed my sketches to Quintilla, Priscilla and Maximilla, who made useful suggestions, and then to craftsmen far more qualified than myself. Not all my ideas were viable, either practically or economically, and were modified accordingly. It was a communal effort. Our white marble church would measure 115 long by 75 feet wide, with the substructure, walls and floor made from marble. The area suffered from periodic earthquakes, so the foundations had to be strong. Entrance to the church would be through large wooden double doors from the west, crossing a massive marble threshold.

We had many helpers; men, women, children, all volunteered to carry stones from the nearby quarry, singing as they went. The slabs from the canyon quarry were fetched by donkey. The quarry workers became interested in our project and offered to deliver loads so they could visit our site and monitor our progress. This saved us making trips to the quarry and speeded our progress. Unfortunately, it also aroused the Romans' suspicion. Their suspicions were further fuelled by some of the quarry workers becoming followers of the New Prophecy movement.

Once the walls were in place, a wooden frame we had constructed, was raised with pulleys onto the tops of the walls. We now had a church roof, with a wooden cross above the door.

I asked one of the stonemasons to make a copy of the Mary

Magdalene statue we had installed at the cave community - she would have pride of place at the front of the church overlooking the congregation.

Meanwhile, I had been making the church pews and altar; so these were put in place as soon as all the stonework was complete. We christened her the 'Church of St Mary', in honour of Mary Magdalene, and held our first service just six months after we had broken soil. We sang so loudly we almost raised the roof!

October 141

Unlike the Catholic church, the Romans had turned a 'blind eye' to our activities up until now. The prosperity and tax revenues of Pepouza had increased since our arrival, so they left us be.

But the building of our white marble church attracted their unwanted attention. They came to interview us to find out how we could have possibly have afforded such an expensive church?

Fortunately, Quintilla had kept accounts detailing every item of expenditure and record of donations. We knew we had enemies keen to see the backs of us by accusing us of some crime, real or invented. But they could find no fault -the accounts were perfectly in order.

This angered them, so they directed their wrath at the quarry workers. They accused them of selling us materials at a discounted price, in exchange for backhanders. This was fabricated and they had no proof, but this did not stop the workers being deemed untrustworthy and losing their jobs, along with their homes.

This saddened me greatly, but in order to protect them I distanced myself -at least their lives were spared. When the Romans left the city, which they eventually would, we would find a way of helping them.

Before they left they dealt us a cruel blow.

One Saturday evening in early October, whilst we were all in church celebrating the marriage of two of our younger members, twenty or so Roman soldiers made their way to our cave community at dusk. Fortunately no one was there, except Amos the donkey.

The Roman soldiers threw oil soaked lit torches at the lowest wooden balcony. The wood was bone dry, as the rains had not yet come, and the flames took hold quickly.

One of the local lads spotted a golden glow of the fire in the distance, and came running into the church shouting "fire! fire!". The music stopped, and I stood there, frozen, confused. The boy shouted out again, urging us to action,

"The cave community is on fire, hurry hurry!"

We raced over there, but by the time we got there, it was too late... the flames had reached the upper levels by then, enveloping the wooden doors I had so lovingly crafted. The lower balcony was already reduced to blackened charred wood, breaking off in places.

Amos had broken free from his tether, kicked down his wooden stall, and somehow scrambled down the steep rocky cliff walls. He was running around, distressed, but still alive, and unharmed.

There was absolutely nothing we could do. The fire had taken hold and the furnace like heat prevented us getting anywhere near. I stood there, rooted to the spot, overwhelmed by feelings of despair and utter desolation. These feelings were familiar to me, and I did not welcome their return. I felt beaten.

I could not bear to watch any longer, so I approached Amos, calming him by talking to him and stroking his face. I was soothing myself actually. I buried my face in his head, sobbing like a child, holding onto him for dear life.

Unbeknown to me, Priscilla, Maximilla, Quintilla and the others, had stood in a circle, holding hands and praying out loud together.

In a few moments, there was a huge clap of thunder, followed by lightning which lit up the star lit sky.

I looked up to see the heavens open and a torrential downpour falling directly over us. This was not the rainy season. The fire on the balconies spluttered and crackled as the rainwater extinguished the flames, enabling us to scramble up the rock face. Most of us had brought cloths soaked with water from the river - we smothered any residual flames with the cloths and stamped on them with our sandaled feet.

We prayed thanks to God for putting the fire out, it was a miracle.

But the smoke made the place uninhabitable. I felt Quintilla's arm around my shoulder,

"Come, Montanus, there is nothing more to be done for now. We should go back to the city and return in the morning." She was right of course... I slowly took Amos by his halter and led him back to the city. I handed him over to the boy who had alerted us, and asked him to take good care of him. I barely heard him excitedly telling me a miracle had taken place - there had been no rain in Pepouza that night.

I wanted to be alone. I retreated to our bedroom - Quintilla sensed this and left me be. I was full of anger and self-pity. My default setting in difficult times. I could not hear God, or any of the angels who are always ready to help us. I could not face anyone anymore. When was New Jerusalem coming anyway? Why had I been led here and invited all these people to join me?

My mind was in overdrive and sleep was out of the question. Dawn came and Quintilla gently knocked on the door to ask if I wanted anything to eat and drink. I declined as I had no appetite or thirst for life.

As I write these words I feel a mixture of shame for accusing God of forsaking me, and incredulity at the total absurdity of the situation. My mind was in control - I had expected God to stop the fire altogether, not just put it out.

A quiet realization slowly dawned on me that it was all part of the human condition to struggle in life - that is the only way we grow. It is mirrored in nature. The vine which grows in the poor soil produces the best wine - the struggle is part of the process and imperative. To surrender to God. Simple but not always easy. We cannot possibly understand the big picture when we are but a grain of sand in the desert. That is where faith and trust come in -to sustain us in difficult times.

I was awakened from my reverie with Quintilla knocking on the door again. We had received word from Myriam and Matilda in Gaul.

When I emerged, dressed and washed, Quintilla greeted me,

"Good morning Montanus, I am pleased to see you are looking much better this morning!" She looked like nothing had happened the night before - I was fortunate to be surrounded by such strong women. No wonder the bishops were fearful of them - they were a force to be reckoned with!

Quintilla sat at the table expectantly, holding Myriam's letter, awaiting my full attention before she would start to read it to me.

30th September 141, Lyons, Gaul

Dear Mother and Father

I am so sorry it has taken me so long to write but we have been so terribly busy here in Gaul. After our wonderful stay in Saintes Maries de la Mer with the du Bois family, we sailed up the river Rhone to Lyons.

Philippe du Bois gave us a letter of introduction to Alexander, a Greek Jewish carpenter living there with his family.

Befitting its importance, Lyons had not one, but two Roman theatres. The larger one seated 10,000 spectators, with the Odeon theatre more intimate, seating just 2,500 people. Alexander invited us to stay with his family, even though they had no idea we were coming and we had arrived unannounced!

Matilda and I are finding the local language a little easier to understand now, although there seem to be countless dialects. Of course, we are at home with the many Greek speaking immigrants from Asia Minor who have come here for a better life.

The people here are a multi-racial cocktail of Ligurians, Iberians, Phoenicians, Celts, plus over 500 tribes from ancient Gaul. So we are just something else to add to the melting pot.

The great River Rhone was the corridor for inland commerce; metal ores, tin and finished metalwork, leather goods and furs came south, while fine ceramics, bronzes, oils, wines and spices were traded north.

The Jewish communities enjoy a higher status here, allowed to own their own properties. Women are able to hold their own land and business, and legacies split evenly between all male and female heirs.

Anyway, when we explained that we had been taught basic carpentry skills by our father and grandfather at Lake Mareotis, Alexander said he had been looking for some extra help, and would be delighted to work with the first two female carpenters in Lyons! So that is what we have been doing, as well as preaching in the wealthy people's homes about the New Prophecy.

We have had a lot of interest from the Greeks from Asia Minor, who had heard of you father, and your work at Pepouza. The local women are most intrigued by us being carpenters, having never encountered females ones before - they are nearly all weavers, as that is considered appropriate work for women to do in their homes.

They also love to hear about our connection with Mary Magdalene, who is legendary in these parts.

Mother, you would just love the music and poetry that is performed in the market squares!

They are called *jongleurs*, travelling musicians and storytellers, who work along the networks of pilgrim roads, performing in the market squares of towns along the roads to Jerusalem, Rome and the tomb of St James at Compostela. They appear on their own, in small bands, or sometimes as a family. They are so talented - they are able to play a vast range of instruments; as well as sing, juggle and sometimes perform acrobatic tricks!

To take to the road as a jongleur automatically set one aside from feudal society; because no loyalty was owed to any single lord or land, they received no protection from feudal law. The downside of this was that any crimes committed against them were considered not to have happened. But what freedom they had, travelling across frontiers into lands of their choice.

The Provencal *troubadours* worked alongside the jongleurs but came from a different class and their influences were Hispano Arabic. *Troubadour* means 'inventor' or 'maker'. They were trained in the skills of war but seldom needed to use them. They had usually received a more liberal education and readily adapted the role of 'poet', seeing themselves as 'musical warriors'.

During the winter months a troubadour would spend time at his ancestral home practising his combat skills and composing new poems, the bulk of which were concerned with chivalry and love - particularly 'ideal' love, a pure emotion having nothing to do with marriage, sexual passion or dynastic ambitions. The beloved is unattainable; she might be married, having taken 'Holy Orders', or even be dead, but nevertheless the lover longs for her and dedicates himself to her.

The troubadour was resistant to dogma and had little sympathy for the Catholic Church. The Cathars, a Christian Gnostic movement originating from the days of Mary Magdalene and her followers, had a firm foothold in the region.

The Cathars did not believe in any church hierarchy or ownership of property, the community was the centre of their faith. At the centre of each community were the male and female Perfects who after baptism had renounced the world for an ascetic life and periods of prayer and fasting. They were known as 'Good Christians'; they did not engage in sexual activity and did not eat meat, cheese, eggs, milk or butter.

Noblewomen, who benefited from independence not enjoyed in other parts of Gaul, founded, managed and led Cathar homes.

In the absence of church buildings, people gathered in homes run by a female Cathar *Perfect** to listen to the visiting male Cathars from the cities.

The locals greeted these quiet, robed, men and women of God by bowing deeply and reciting a prayer that asked for assurance of a good end to their lives. This ritual, known as the *melioramentum*, marked the supplicants as believers in the Cathar message. These believers, or *credentes,* were not strictly speaking practising Cathars, but sympathizers who bore witness and showed deference to the faith.

Then in the evening, the troubadours and jongleurs would come to entertain the same people who had been uplifted by the Cathars in the afternoon.

There was a bond and feeling of mutual respect between them.

In spring, the troubadours would set out on horseback with a troupe of jongleurs, visiting the lords and aristocrats, presenting new works which might be put into manuscript form and presented as gifts.

---

* Perfects - the spiritual elite of Catharism, they come from any social caste. After three years of training, they become vegetarian and are bound to a life of chastity & charity.

Few of the lords could play an instrument, so they employed male and female jongleurs to create musical settings for their poems. Some lords became so immersed in the troubadour tradition, they bankrupted themselves by buying fabulous outfits, giving rich gifts and paying vast numbers of jongleurs.

Louis de Troyes was a well known troubadour; when he came to the market square in Lyons, word quickly spread and people would come from miles around to be entertained. Matilda and I would often be there also, preaching the New Prophecy.

When he was not performing, Louis stood at the back, listening to what we had to say. He had many questions, and was clearly intrigued. He was also very interested in Matilda. Louis was handsome, of course, but they tended not to be the marrying kind, and we were not looking for suitors, needless to say. Matilda is enthralled by his poems; she is so like Mother, poetry speaks to her soul, and her face lights up when he speaks. He in turn responds to her bright, lilting laugh, that rings through the air, as clear as a bell, with genuine merriment.

I know nothing of courtship, but I can see they have a strong connection... Louis has composed poems for Matilda, and reads them out loud to the crowds, all the time looking at Matilda. At first she blushed, but then she started to respond with words of her own - she was in her element. The crowd loved it of course - a real life unscripted love story in action!

When we retired to our lodgings, I would tease Matilda as any older sister would - she flatly denied any feelings for Louis, but her denial was unconvincing.

Autumn came, and Louis returned to his family estate, to prepare for the following year. So that was that, Matilda had said, flatly, with a hint of a sigh. I was not convinced.

So how is everything at Pepouza? The cave community? The new church? Prisca and Maximilla? Matilda asked me to send an extra big hug to Prisca - and to tell her she would love it here!

We think of you often and miss you terribly, but we feel our efforts are being rewarded here, our house groups are growing so rapidly that some of our members have suggested we build a church here in Lyons - wouldn't that be amazing?

We have met a man called Pothinus, who comes from Asia Minor. He is a similar age to father, and he wants to help us. I had a dream that he would be the first Bishop of Lyons - imagine that?

Anyway, we must make haste, we have commissions to finish!

Send our love and blessings to everyone,

Myriam and Matilda xxxxxx

I sat there for a few minutes, digesting the girls' news. Quintilla looked delighted, I less so.

Yes, they were safe and had settled in well - I was thankful for that. Less welcome was the prospect that Matilda was falling in love with a street musician. He better hadn't break my daughter's heart, or maybe it would be better in the long run? My mind ran away with various scenarios... Quintilla looked at my worried face and gently took hold of my hand,

"Do not fret my love, the girls will be just fine. Remember how my parents reacted to you? They have to make their own choices - all we can do is pray, surrender and trust that all will be well." Quintilla was right of course, she normally was. She also suggested we keep this latest news from Priscilla and Maximilla. Nothing was certain yet and we did not wish to hurt Priscilla unnecessarily.

If Matilda did marry this travelling poet, Priscilla would be devastated - it would only confirm her worst fears of not seeing Matilda again.

I would not be overjoyed myself.

Chapter XXII

New Beginnings

March 142

We spent the winter in Pepouza in our house adjoining the church. We planned to restore the cave community in the spring, when our spirits were restored and the rainy season was over.

It was a valuable time for reflection, and we decided to consolidate our efforts with the church here in Pepouza. To this aim, we set up a hierarchy aligned with the Catholic Church; the appointment of a bishop, deacons and presbyters.

Many people came to us disillusioned with the Catholic Church; we honoured all Christian beliefs, but there were stark differences. We did not believe the church officers held the keys to the church, or the power of forgiveness. That preserve was for God alone. We also did not believe you needed a church intermediary to have a relationship with God. That was up to the individual and for him or her alone.

We had an equal division between men and women - all were equal in the eyes of God. The statue of Mary Magdalene stood at the front of the church to remind us how it all began - we would not be here without her lifetime's work after Yeshua died. We were not in opposition to anybody - we advocated loving one's neighbour. Everyone was entitled to their beliefs - we were all individuals and yet we were all One... We prayed for peace, just as the Essenes had done.

The Catholic Church's main criticism of us was that we claimed the Holy Spirit worked through us, inducing 'frenzied states' which 'duped' our congregations. This was grossly exaggerated of course. We were also accused of cannibalism and incest - this was preposterous! These were just diversions - the main problem was over our treatment of women.

They did not admit to it, but some, not all, bishops found it inconceivable that women could hold positions of office - this was abhorrent in their eyes and had to be stopped at any cost. The delayed arrival of the New Jerusalem at Pepouza did not in any way slow the growth of the New Prophecy, or Montanist movement as it was now being called.

Restoration of the cave community got underway, starting with the rebuilding of the balconies, so we could gain access to all three levels. It was easier the second time round as we had learned from experience, and we sang hymns as we happily worked alongside one another.

Then it was time to clean up inside as best we could - we removed all the charred wooden remains before scrubbing the floors, walls and ceilings. We put them in a huge pile outside to set alight when we were ready to rechristen our cave community - a new start.

Of course the caves themselves were not damaged, some of the cave roofs and crosses we had engraved in the walls were charred - we left them like that as a salutary reminder of our enemies. We would pray for them, that they would see the error of their ways; this was the only way, and what Yeshua had taught us.

The third level with the baptismal pools and my room was the least damaged, the sudden downpour together with the pools of water acting as a firebreak, preserved the wooden ceilings and fittings.

Summer came and we were ready to move back into the cave community - the church officers we had elected in the winter were able to run our church in Pepouza. We were not fearful of the Romans and any future attacks, but we took the precaution of having someone there all the time on watch, just as we did at Lake Mareotis.

I split my time between the cave community and Pepouza - the caves were my retreat - where I felt renewed. I would wake at dawn and stand on my balcony, watching the sun come up over the horizon. It never failed to fill me with awe - I felt close to God there.

October 142

Quintilla came hurrying to find me at the cave community with another letter from Myriam clasped in her hand. She always waited for me before reading her letters, so we could hear our daughters' news together.

16th September 142

Dear Mother and Father

We have the most marvellous news - Louis and Matilda are to be married on 30th September! By the time you receive this letter they will be man and wife! I can't quite believe it! It all happened so quickly - and it was so romantic!

One day last month, Louis galloped into the market square, leapt down off his horse, and got down on one knee in front of Matilda. He took her left hand and said if she did not marry him he would fall on his sword!

We, and the people around, thought it was just a charade at first, and Matilda stood there open-mouthed, not sure whether to laugh or cry!

But the look on Louis' face was so earnest, with such love in his eyes, Matilda just looked at him and said yes! Louis placed a simple silver band on her wedding finger as a sign of their betrothal, and then gently kissed it.

The crowd applauded and cheered - the love story they had been witnessing had a happy ending. They will be married in Lyons registry office and then Matilda wants a 'Song of Songs' ceremony, the ancient love poem from the Jewish scriptures that legend says Queen Sheba gave to King Solomon. This is what our great grandparents Sarah and Jean Claude had at their wedding in Saintes Maries de la Mer in 56.

It is what Sarah's parents, Mary Magdalene and Yeshua would have had if Yeshua had survived. The bride and bridegroom anoint one another before entering the Bride's secret chamber and open to one another in preparation for conceiving a child in a space of love and light.

Matilda told Louis she could not simply abandon her duties here in Lyons, so intends to spend the winters here in Lyons with me, and the summers travelling with Louis. How exciting is that? I told Matilda that unlike her, I am able to live alone and she should be with her husband, but she just waved her hand dismissively, saying she couldn't just give up what we were doing, and anyway didn't want to leave me.

In fact she said I should learn a musical instrument and travel with them. Of course, I have no intention of gallivanting around the countryside with them.

We now have a church where we can assemble - Pothinus acquired a disused storehouse that we have hastily restored. Matilda and I made the wooden pews, altar, font and cross. Humble beginnings, but more and more people are coming each week!

How are Prisca and Maximilla? We both miss you all terribly - why don't you come and visit soon? I must go -

With love, light and blessings

Myriam and Matilda

xxxx

Quintilla hands shook as she read the letter, her voice getting faster and louder as she became increasingly excited. I don't think I have ever seen her look so happy... her skin glistened in the sunlight, every pore in her body seemed to exude delight. I knew why, of course.

Our younger daughter Matilda had married a travelling poet; poetry had been a life long passion of hers.

Quintilla had come back to me, and was a loyal and faithful wife, but poetry was what made her heart and soul sing.

I did not feel betrayed. I understood. We were both born under Gemini, the sign of the twins. We both knew that the only person who we truly confided in was our other self.

My mind turned to the practicalities of Matilda's married life, but I knew I would be wasting my breath raising these with Quintilla. It was not the time to share my doubts that were mere projections from my mind. Love *can* conquer all. I looked at my dear wife - I had never seen her so happy - her dreams had been realised through our daughter. She kept singing out loud, whilst dancing around the room,

"My daughter has married a poet, my daughter has married a poet..." over and over.

February 156 - Polycarp's Martyrdom

I received a letter from Irenaeus* relating the sad news of Polycarp's martyrdom. Irenaeus was from Smyrna and as a young man, after hearing the preaching of Polycarp, became a Christian and one of his disciples.

Irenaeus said that Polycarp had spoken fondly of me; and would have wished for Irenaeus to write personally to me with a full account of his martyrdom. As Irenaeus had been in Rome at the time, Polycarp's assistant, Marcianus, had witnessed his martyrdom and summarised the course of events.

Polycarp was of a great age, in his 100th year; Christians were being rounded up by the Romans and so his companions urged him to seek refuge in a remote farm some distance from Smyrna, where he prayed day and night for all men and churches throughout the world.

*Irenaeus would become the first great Christian theologian.

Whilst praying, he fell into a trance and saw his pillow burning with fire. He interpreted this as a sign that he would be burned alive. Two farm hands were captured by the police and under torture, revealed his whereabouts.

Herod, the captain of police, was eager to bring Polycarp into the stadium to make a spectacle of him. Herod sent gendarmes and horsemen late one evening to arrest him. When they arrived, Polycarp invited them in and ordered a spread of food and drink to be laid on for them. Polycarp persuaded the men to allow him to pray for an hour; he prayed for two hours, remembering everyone who had come his way, small and great, high and low, and all the Universal Church throughout the world. The police were amazed, at both his fitness and grace, saying they had never come across such a respectable, wise old man. They wondered why Herod was so keen to have this old man arrested.

When Polycarp had finished his prayers, they seated him on an ass and led him into the city of Smyrna. It was a high Sabbath, Saturday 22nd February 156.

He was met by Herod and his father, Nicetes, who invited Polycarp into their carriage, saying to him,

"What harm is there in saying 'Caesar is Lord' and offering incense? It would save your life." Polycarp answered,

"I am not going to do what you advise me to do". Herod persisted, but when they failed to persuade him, they pushed him out of the carriage, so that he stumbled and bruised his shin. He promptly got up, and without turning around, was briskly escorted to the stadium, full of a roaring crowd baying for his blood.

The magistrate said to Polycarp,

"With respect for your great age, swear the oath, and I will release you; renounce Christ". Polycarp answered,

"For all the years have I been his servant, and He has done me no wrong. How can I abandon and blaspheme my King and Saviour?"

The crowd shouted out that Polycarp should be burned alive, just as he had predicted. A pile was made ready, and Polycarp was tied and bound to a stake. He looked up to the heavens and said,

"O Lord God Almighty, Father of your beloved and blessed Son Christ. I bless you for granting me this day and hour, so that in the company of martyrs, I may share the cup of Christ and resurrection of eternal life, both of soul and of body, in the incorruptibility of the Holy Spirit. May I be received as a rich and acceptable sacrifice, as you did prepare and reveal it, and have accomplished it. You are the faithful and true God. For this cause, and for all things I praise you, I bless you, I glorify you, through the eternal and heavenly Christ, your beloved Son. Amen."

When he had finished his prayer the fire was lit. A mighty flame flashed up, but the fire, like a sail filled by the wind, made a wall around his body. Instead of the smell of flesh burning, there was a fragrant scent of frankincense in the air.

So the executioners, seeing that he could not be burnt to death, stepped forward and stabbed him with a spear. A dove flew up as he expired.

Our Christian friends were not allowed to take his body away, in case 'we abandoned the crucified one and began to worship this man', and the centurion threw his body into the middle of the fire. They waited for the fire to cool and gathered his bones, which were more valuable than precious stones and finer than refined gold. They laid them to rest at the church he had been bishop of for most of his life.

So the blessed Polycarp, who along with 11 others from Philadelphia suffered martyrdom in Smyrna, is especially remembered by all men, both Christians and heathens, for he showed himself not only a gifted teacher, but also a courageous martyr.

I was pleased to have met Polycarp, a truly remarkable man. I did not possess the strength of character he showed repeatedly throughout his 99 years...

But as I approached my 70th birthday, I was learning not to feel guilty about my flaws - all we can do is do the best we can - they are part of who we are, and at least helps one to be more compassionate to others' failings.

The years rolled by and life continued at Pepouza - the New Prophecy movement continued to grow and had reached Africa. New Jerusalem still failed to appear at Pepouza, but our faith was steadfast.

Priscilla and Maximilla were gifted preachers; articulate, reasoned and well respected. They were shining examples of the Divine Feminine at work; I was happy to step back and spend time at the cave community. Quintilla stayed mostly at the house in Pepouza, supervising our church and community.

Proculus travelled to Rome in 160 and spread the word there. We had been tolerated from a distance; the bishops had written to the Pope since our arrival complaining about our so called sacrilegious behaviours, but he had always turned a blind eye, clearly not believing we were against the Christian Church.

Proculus' arrival in Rome forced the Pope to reluctantly intervene and the 'First official manifestation again Montanists' was issued.

Propaganda and misinformation maintained our movement was a blatant attack on the Catholic faith; in 177, the bishops of Asia Minor gathered in synods and finally succeeded in excommunicating us. We became a separate sect governed from Pepouza, just as we started.

Shortly after, I was gazing out from my balcony one sunny morning when I had an epiphany. I was in my 90th year, and had been waiting for the arrival of New Jerusalem for 40 years.

We prophesied with the blessing of the Holy Spirit - the Spirit moved of its own freewill, and could not be contained in temples and churches. We did not need bricks and mortar, or jewel encrusted walls, as predicted in *Revelation*.

Pepouza was our spiritual centre, and had been for the last 40 years.

I smiled to myself. I had been blind - it had been staring me in the face.

A feeling of peace washed over me as I realized New Jerusalem was already here.

Chapter XXIII

Myriam's Note

September 177: Farewell to Montanus

Matilda and I were on our way back to Pepouza - Mother had written to us to say that Father was seriously unwell and he wanted to see us. She said they lived at the church house in Pepouza now, as it was more comfortable for them.

It was over 30 years since we had left Pepouza - so much had happened.

Our Christian community in Lyons had suffered a most awful tragedy earlier that year. In the early days, we had been left alone more or less, with persecution restricted to the odd verbal assault or threatened stoning. The Caesars were largely content to treat Christianity as a local problem, and leave it to their local Roman officials to deal with. So, our treatment depended on the mood and favour of the Roman governor of Gaul. First, we were forbidden from the marketplace, then the forum, the public baths and finally in any public places. If we did appear in public, we were mocked, beaten, and robbed by the mob. Our homes were vandalized.

Louis heard that there was going to be a mass arrest, and begged Matilda, the children and myself to leave Lyons and take refuge in the countryside with friends of his. Louis was well known, and had friends everywhere.

Pothinus was the same age as Father and I was reluctant to leave him, he had been like a father to me during our time in Lyons, we had become close after Matilda's marriage.

Matilda persuaded me - she never missed an opportunity of airing her clever wits - diplomatic and calm, but steely at the same time. She won me over by reminding me we had to protect the next generation - they were the *sang raal*, the Holy Blood line of Yeshua and Mary Magdalene.

Matilda and Louis had two children, Joshua was born in 145, and Marie in 147. Joshua had recently married Blanche, a Cathar sympathiser who owned her own home. Marie was betrothed to Alfonso, a troubadour from Catalonia. So the bloodline would continue...

The family normally congregated in Lyons for a reunion in the autumn, after the troubadours had finished their tour. But it was not safe for us to remain in Lyon, so we left the city to take refuge in the country with Louis' friends - we would be prepared to move at a moment's notice, as the Romans were relentless and may well have offered a reward for our heads.

Eventually, the authorities seized as many Christians as they could and questioned them in the amphitheatre in front of the crowds. They were accused of *"Thyestean banquets and Oedipean intercourse,"* or cannibalism and incest. These utterly inconceivable accusations were denied and so they were imprisoned until the arrival of the Roman governor.

Irenaeus, who had written to father after the martyrdom of Polycarp, originally from Asia Minor, was now a presbyter in a Christian community in the neighbouring town Vienne.

He was sent with a letter, written by some of the Church of Lyons members awaiting martyrdom, to Pope Eleutherus pleading for mercy.

When the governor arrived, he interrogated the Christians in front of the crowds once again, much to the delight of the onlookers.

Bishop Pothinus was beaten and scourged, and died shortly after in prison. A slave, Blandina, was subjected to extreme torture. She was hung on a stake to be the food of beasts, but none of the beasts would touch her. She was taken back to prison, and then cast in a net and thrown before a bull.

Eleutherus refused to intervene. In the end, all 48 were killed, half of them were of Greek origin, half Gallo-Roman. It was a dark day in Lyons for the Christian community.

Irenaeus returned and succeeded Pothinus as bishop of Lyons. He wrote letters to Eleutherus and the bishops in Asia Minor, giving the names of 48 of their number who had suffered martyrdom.

The Pope listened. His letters resulted in a virtual amnesty for Christians as long as Eleutherus was in office. Irenaeus was of sharp mind and strong faith; the Christian community licked its wounds and carried on as before, but without the fear of persecution, grew rapidly. Many of the onlookers, who had witnessed the barbaric treatment of the Lyons Christians in the amphitheatre, were so impressed by their ability to withstand pain and torture, not least the miracle they witnessed with the slave girl Blandina, they became Christians.

We were greeted by the faithful Theodutus, who Father had appointed as financial officer 40 years ago. With Father's failing health, he had been appointed as leader of the community.

Mother and Maximilla were there too; Prisca had gone to the light a few years earlier. She went to sleep one night and never woke up - she was 70 years old. I felt a pang of remorse as I remembered her words when we left. She had been right - we never did return to her. Both Prisca and Maximilla had asked to be buried alongside Montanus ; three tombs awaited them in the church grounds in Pepouza.

When her time came, Quintilla would be buried alongside her husband, Montanus.

We tiptoed into Father's, not wishing to awaken him. He looked lifeless, grey in colour, with slow, laboured breathing. He failed to open his eyes. I could feel my throat tighten with emotion, as I looked at the Father I remembered, reduced to a lifeless skeleton. I was crying inside, but I held back the tears - Father would not wish us to cry for him - he often said what a wonderful life he had had.

Matilda and I sat either side of his bed, each holding one of his cool, bony, hands. There was a smell of death in the room.

"Father, it's Myriam", I whispered in his ear, while gently squeezing his hand. "He has not been awake for some days now", Mother said, to warn me of there being no response. To my surprise, Father squeezed my hand almost imperceptibly, struggling to open his eyes. He seemed to muster all his remaining effort to utter the next few words,

"Ah, my daughters have returned...", with a smile appearing at the corners of his parched lips. He pointed at Mother and then at me,

"Please, give her the diaries" he gasped almost inaudibly. Mother interjected, "Montanus, you must rest and save your strength!", but it was too late, he had gone... He closed his eyes and after a long pause, exhaled his last breath.

We laid father to rest in the place he had loved from the moment he had set his eyes on 40 years earlier, Pepouza. Mother told me he had always felt overshadowed by his father Jude, with his gift for writing. But Father had started his own community, which was thriving and continued to dominate Asia Minor and beyond.

But he had done much more. For Matilda and I, he was the most wonderful father we could ever have wished for. He never criticized, only encouraged us to follow our hearts and souls, every moment of each day, as long as we lived. He did not judge us, but empowered us to make our own decisions. Quite simply, he believed in us. He would be in our hearts forever, and his light would illuminate and guide us as long as we walked the earth.

Mother honoured his final request and retrieved the diaries of my grandfather, Jude, and father, John Julius (or Montanus) from a strong box in the church cellar. They were in the old battered satchel he had inherited from his father Jude.

She silently handed them to me for safekeeping.

She did not need to tell me to guard them with my life.

Matilda and I prepared to leave for Gaul once again. This was our home now.

It was also where Mary Magdalene's bloodline was continuing; the diaries would be safely hidden and passed down through her chosen descendants.

They would be revealed when the time was right, to those who had eyes to see and ears to hear...

EPILOGUE

For 400 years, Pepouza would remain the centre of the New Prophecy or as it came to be known, the Montanist movement. It continued in the East until the Roman Emperor Justinian I (527-565) essentially destroyed it, although remnants of it survived until the 9th century.

Montanists were more strict than most Christians in their ethical practices, but one part of their practice was too liberal for the Orthodox Church. Their treatment of women. Montanism encouraged women to participate fully in all aspects of the movement – even as prophetesses and church officers. This was their main objection and why every effort was made to stamp it out.

In 550, under the orders of Justinian, John of Ephesus, as part of an attempt to root out all *heretics, pagans and Jews* in the provinces of Asia Minor, destroyed the shrine in Pepouza containing the bones of Montanus, Priscilla, Maximilla, and another Montanist prophetess (possibly Quintilla). He also confiscated all Montanist buildings in the city, turning them over to the orthodox Christian church for its use.

The Lake Mareotis community survived until the 7th century; one day the Leader received angelic guidance that their work was done there, for now.

The wooden buildings would decay and return to Mother Earth, leaving no proof of their existence for over 600 years... The diaries had been safely buried centuries ago; they had few possessions, so they left leaving only their footprints behind in the sand, just as the Essenes had done at Qumran in 68.

By 1200, there were over 1000 Perfects in the Languedoc region. The Cathars were an obvious threat to the Church, they did not revere saintly relics; in their eyes the church was the work of evil as it encouraged violence, and since the Church was corrupt, the Church Sacraments were worthless.

In 1198, Innocent II was elected as Pope and was determined to stop what he saw as the public humiliation of the Church by the Cathars. 12,000 mounted knights, infantry, archers and an unknown number of mercenaries, assembled at Lyons on 22 July 1209, the feast day of Mary Magdalene.

They attacked Beziers, the Cathar stronghold, and put 20,000 to the sword. Thousands of men and women in other towns were burned alive. Carcassonne was starved out - the lands were granted to Simon de Montfort who began a systematic take-over of Languedoc. Those who escaped fled to Montsegur in the Pyrenees, to Toulouse, or to the castles of sympathetic nobility. Jews were dispossessed and the southern heiresses forced to take northern husbands. It was nothing less than genocide.

In my 'story', the bloodline of Yeshua and Mary Magdalene continues in Gaul, which later became France. Even in France today, many people are convinced of this. Critics say there is no proof, and one answer to this is that most of it was destroyed during the slaughter of the Cathar movement.

Fortunately there were survivors, including the children of Joshua and Marie, who carried on the line, initially in Gaul and Catalonia. They migrated, but that is another story...

As a consequence, there are now over a million people in the world today who are descended from Jesus and Mary Magdalene, of all creeds and colour. I am not one of them, but *you* may well be...

Mary Magdalene was an extraordinary woman, who I have learned much about through reading the Gnostic gospels. She was airbrushed out of history by the Orthodox Church, portrayed as a repentant sinner, whereas in the Gnostic gospels she was revered as a leader, priestess, teacher, healer and mother.

And for a woman as great as her, it is not surprising to discover she had the last word, literally. Her final legacy will send shock waves through the Orthodox Church. My cellular memory tells me that 9 out of the 27 books of the New Testament were written by Mary

Magdalene under pseudonyms (see page 252).

What a perfectly sweet irony, to hide under the guise of men in order for her writings to be accepted by the Church?

I possess none of Mary Magdalene's qualities; but I do have a passionate desire to discover the Universal Truth. For some reason, I have been guided to shine a light in a dark corner of religious his-tory, to bring awareness to her-story, one of the greatest injustices against women of all time.

So, I can hear you ask if this story is actually *true*?

Dr David R Hawkins (1927-2012), an eminent psychiatrist, co-authored Orthomolecular Psychiatry with Nobel Laureate chemist Linus Paul in 1973; it was a ground-breaking piece of work that initiated a new field within psychiatry.

He studied consciousness and established a few core principles:-

Love is more powerful than hatred, truth sets us free, forgiveness liberates both sides, unconditional love heals, courage empowers, and the essence of Divinity is peace.

After 250,000 muscle testing calibrations and multiple research studies over 30 years at the Institute of Advanced Spiritual Research, he developed a Map of Consciousness. This Map of Consciousness incorporated findings from quantum physics and nonlinear dynamics, categorising the stages of spiritual evolution described in sacred texts. His quest was to assist human spiritual evolution.

He found that consciousness (energy fields) could be calibrated on a scale of 1-1000. At the low end of the scale are Guilt (30), Fear (100), Anger (150). All levels above 200 are described as "Power"; Power is always manifested with grace. Grace is associated with humility. Higher on the scale are Courage (200), Willingness (310), Reason (400) and Love (500). Humans at these levels recognize they are the source of their own lives.

At the highest end of the scale (700-1000) are qualities that transcend duality. The oral teachings of the great prophets of human history - Jesus, Krishna and Buddha, all calibrate at 1000. Unfortunately, their message was recorded by followers lower on the scale; in Christian teachings, by the 2nd century the level of truth was at 930 but by the 6th century it had dropped to 540. Interestingly, the recorded teachings of Buddha calibrate the highest ranging from 850 -960.

According to Hawkins, in 2006 there were only three people on the planet who calibrated over 700. Hawkins also says 85% of the planet register below 200, counterbalanced by the 15% above 200. Furthermore, one individual over 700 counterbalances 70 million individuals below 200! Without these counterbalances, mankind would self-destruct from unopposed negativity. We only have to look around to see the future of humanity is more precarious than ever.

The contents of this book have been independently tested by a kinesiologist and calibrate at 950. This is because the gnostic gospels, the secret teachings of Jesus, and the whole essence of this book, were written in the 1st and 2nd centuries, preserved intact, and not discovered until the 20th century!

Clearly, the words came *through me*, not from me; I firmly believe that Ratu Bagus enabled this process. My gratitude to him knows no bounds.

This is a story, but it also appears to be the Universal Truth.

BOOKS OF THE NEW TESTAMENT

1 **Matthew**
2 **Mark**
3 **Luke**
4 **John**
5 **Acts**
6 Romans
7 1 Corinthians
8 2 Corinthians
9 Galatians
10 Ephesians
11 Philippians
12 Colossians
13 1 Thessalonians
14 2 Thessalonians
15 1 Timothy
16 2 Timothy
17 Titus
18 Philemon
19 **Hebrews**
20 **James**
21 **1 Peter**
22 **2 Peter**
23 1 John
24 2 John
25 3 John
26 Jude
27 Revelation

Those highlighted in **bold** were written by Mary Magdalene; Matthew, Mark and Luke were written in collaboration with the apostles

YESHUA AND MARY MAGDALENE'S DESCENDANTS

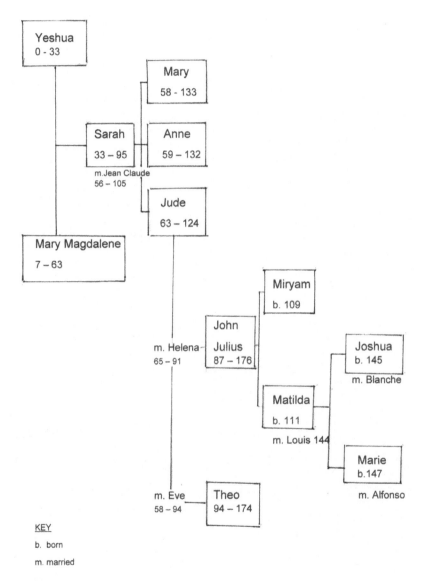

KEY

b. born

m. married

Figure 14: Yeshua and Mary Magdalene's descendants

MARY MAGDALENE'S FINAL LEGACY

Where did Yeshua and Mary Magdalene's line carry on?

Sequel to Mary Magdalene's Legacy, Mary Magdalene's Final Legacy follows the next three generations of Yeshua and Mary Magdalene; through the diaries of Jude, their grandson, and John Julius, their great grandson.

The story takes place in Egypt, Italy, Greece, Asia Minor (Turkey) and Gaul in the 1st and 2nd centuries. Jude suffers a spiritual crisis, and is beset with personal tragedy, but continues with his divine gift, writing.

Jude's son, John Julius, succeeds Jude and then travels to Asia Minor, where he changes his name and founds a new movement which would survive for centuries.

Archaeological discoveries made in the last twenty years together with the unearthing of more ancient Greek papyrus fragments form the basis for this story. These early Christian writings were written under pseudonyms and until now were unconnected with Mary Magdalene's descendants.

Mary Magdalene leaves one final legacy which will send shock waves through the church today...

ALSO BY JULIE DE VERE HUNT

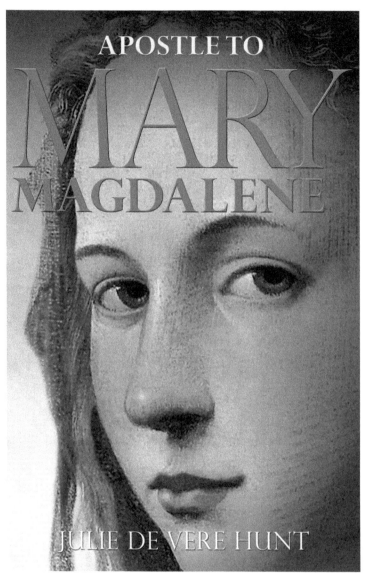

APOSTLE TO
MARY MAGDALENE

JULIE DE VERE HUNT

'Apostle to Mary Magdalene' is an overview in A-Z format of what we know about Mary Magdalene from religious scholars gleaned from the New Testament gospels and the more controversial gnostic gospels discovered in the 20th century. It also touches on metaphysical phenomena such as the Akashic Records, Cellular Memory, Meditation and the Zero Point Field as ways forward to establish the truth.

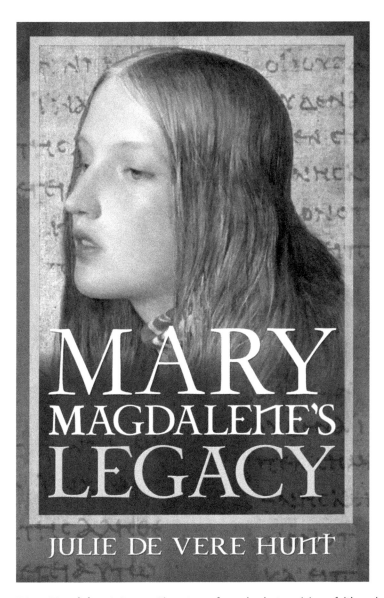

'Mary Magdalene's Legacy' is a story of murder, betrayal, love, faith and courage that rewrites biblical history. It follows the life of Mary Magdalene after the crucifixion, carrying on the bloodline of Jesus and transmitting his original teachings.